Treating Depressed Children

A Therapeutic Manual of Cognitive Behavioral Interventions

Charma D. Dudley, Ph.D.

New Harbinger Publications

Publisher's Note

This publication is designed to provide accurate and authoritative information in regard to the subject matter covered. It is sold with the understanding that the publisher is not engaged in rendering pyschological, financial, legal, or other professional services. If expert assistance or counseling is needed, the services of a competent professional should be sought.

Copyright © 1997 Charma D. Dudley
New Harbinger Publications, Inc.
5674 Shattuck Avenue
Oakland, CA 94609

Edited by Farrin Alyse Jacobs.
Text design by Tracy Marie Powell.
Art by David Turner.

Distributed in U.S.A. by Publishers Group West; in Canada by Raincoast Books; in Great Britain by Airlift Book Company, Ltd.; in South Africa by Real Books, Ltd.; in Australia by Boobook; in New Zealand by Tandem Press.

Library of Congress Catalog Card Number: 96-70515

ISBN 1-57224-061-X paperback

10 9 8 7 6 5 4 3 2

This book is dedicated to my family and friends, who provided me with ongoing support, encouragement, love, friendship, and prayers during this remarkable period in my life. Thanks for standing behind me and giving me that extra nudge, push, or pep talk when I needed it most. You know who you are.

Life's completeness and
richness depend on the things
we share with our loved ones and friends

—Helen Steiner Rice

Contents

Table of Creative Experiments

Foreword

Until recently, it was thought that children and adolescents did not experience clinical depression. It was assumed that children were not cognitively mature enough to develop clinical depression and that adolescents were just going through "growing pains." However, several studies have demonstrated that children and adolescents do have symptoms of depression similar to those experienced by adults (Kovacs 1996). In fact, clinical, as well as epidemiological studies, have shown that approximately 2 percent of children and 6 percent of adolescents may suffer from clinically significant depression. Furthermore, since the second World War, clinical depression seems to be more prevalent and is manifesting itself at earlier ages. Clinically significant depression, usually called major depression and dysthymia, has been demonstrated to be a recurrent disorder that conveys increased risk for suicide, other psychiatric disorders, substance abuse, and impairment of the academic, social, and family functioning of the child.

Several psychotherapeutic and pharmacological methods have been shown to be useful for the acute treatment and prevention of recurrences of major depression. Among these interventions, cognitive behavioral treatment, either individually or as a group, has been found to be particularly useful.

In this easy-to-read, complete, and practical book, Dr. Dudley has summarized the theory of cognitive therapy. She has presented the material taking into account the development of the child and has given multiple useful examples for clinicians who work with depressed youth.

Treating Depressed Children presents twelve sessions of cognitive treatment. It begins with a session on psychoeducation regarding depression, feelings, and cognitive therapy, and graduates to sessions helping the child identify problematic situations, monitor thoughts, change cognitive distortions, improve self-esteem, and identify automatic negative thoughts. The book also teaches relaxation techniques, social skills, how to prevent negative thoughts, and helps the child to continue practicing new ways of thinking after the therapy is over. Each chapter is accompanied by practical examples and excellent drawings that help the child recognize his or her own feeling. There are also useful rating scales to be used by the clinician as well as the child.

Dr. Dudley has prepared a thorough and practical manual that can be used by mental health workers, parents, and children to explore the effects of cognitive therapy on early-onset depression.

— Boris Birmaher, M.D.

Acknowledgments

If someone would have told me back in 1988 when I started utilizing cognitive therapy techniques with children during group and individual therapy that I would someday write a book on this subject, I would have said, "Who me? No way." I did know, however, even back in graduate school that I preferred the cognitive behavioral approach to other treatments. This was mainly due to the fact that I personally preferred more active/directive forms of treatment. In all honesty I had difficulty being nondirective. Back then I had the tendency to ask a lot of "what if" and "how do you know" questions. When I began working with adolescents, and children in particular, I realized that I had to be creative in utilizing cognitive therapy concepts with this population. My background in drama therapy prepared me in many ways to be spontaneous in my work with children. I will never forget the ten-year-old boy who gave me the idea for my first creative experiment, "Enemy Camp vs. Enemy Destroyers." I was trying to explain the concepts of rational and irrational responses in a concrete manner when he brilliantly stated, "It's like a video game—the good guys can nuke the bad guys."

There have been many individuals who have been supportive of me during this process. I would like to thank my friend and colleague, Kim Poling, Program Director of the Services for Teens At Risk (STAR) program at Western Psychiatric Institute and Clinic (Pittsburgh, PA.) for the support, insight, and knowledge she shared with me throughout this project. Kim has extensive training in the field of depression, suicidality, and cognitive therapy with adolescents. She was instrumental in reviewing the manuscript and provided me with a lot of helpful suggestions and feedback. I would not have completed the project without her support. Many heartfelt thanks also go to my friend Brenadette Bryant, a Nurse Educator at Mercy Hospital (Pittsburgh, PA.) who also reviewed the manuscript with an "objective eye" when I couldn't be objective any longer. Brenadette admitted that she didn't know anything about cognitive therapy, but after reviewing the book she was able to reiterate the basic concepts. It felt good when she stated, "Kids can really understand this good and bad self-talk."

My appreciation is also extended to Dr. Boris Birmaher, Medical Director of the Child/Adolescent Mood Disorders Module, Western Psychiatric Institute and Clinic, who graciously agreed to do the foreword for this manuscript despite his own busy schedule that includes assessment, treatment, research and his own writing project. I give credit to Dr. Birmaher for further enhancing my understanding of affective disorders in children. He also encouraged me to write down my creative ideas when I was under his supervision as a Senior Psychiatric Clinician at Western Psychiatric Institute and Clinic.

Writing down these ideas eventually paid off when I had the courage to contact Dr. Matthew McKay from New Harbinger Publications while I was at the APA Convention in New York. I was thrilled when he expressed an interest in my book. Without his initial interest and encouragement my draft would still be on my bookshelf collecting dust. I would also like to thank Farrin Jacobs and Gayle Zanca, at New Harbinger Publications for their patience and ability to put up with a novice writer. I congratulate you both for an excellent job.

I am especially grateful to all those individuals who helped me with typing, editing, computer problems, etc., during this project.

Finally, I would like to thank David Turner, my cousin, friend, and illustrator who provided the artwork for this manuscript. He was able to take my ideas and develop those wonderful pictures that make this manuscript user-friendly for children and mental health professionals alike.

Introduction

Depression is being recognized as a significant problem in the area of child psychology and psychiatry. This manual is for mental health practitioners who work with children exhibiting symptoms of depression, particularly low self-esteem, faulty patterns of thinking (distortions), and social skills deficits.

It outlines a step-by-step treatment package utilizing cognitive behavioral techniques that have been primarily used with adult populations. This manual is targeted for children between the ages of ten and fourteen years old, but can easily be modified for younger children and older adolescents. In general, the word *children* includes the full age range except where a distinction between children and adolescents must be made.

Depression in Children

The question of how depression in childhood should be defined has created much controversy over the years. However, the major features have been agreed upon and include

- Dysphoric mood as usually indicated by sad facial expression

- Self-disclosure or report of sad feelings or hopelessness

- Irritability or anger

- Loss of appetite or failure to obtain normal weight gain

- Increased appetite or weight gain

- Psychomotor agitation or retardation

- Fatigue or tremendous loss of energy

- Feelings of guilt

- Low self-esteem

- Poor concentration or forgetfulness

o Suicidal ideation or suicide attempts

o A change in school performance

o Social avoidance or withdrawal

o Somatic complaints (for example, headaches, stomachaches)

o Social skills deficits

o Negative self-statements or negative self-reinforcements (Frame and Cuddy 1989; Lewinsohn 1978)

Statistics show that at least 10 percent of all American children suffer from depression, although many of the symptoms go unrecognized or unobserved (Nissen 1986). However, other literature indicates that the rates range from 0.4 percent to 8.3 percent with a two-to-one female-to-male ratio in adolescents. For younger children, depression occurs at an equivalent rate in boys and girls (Birmaher, et al. 1996).

While research on depression in children is beginning to emerge, the majority of it has focused on phenomenological features of depression, as well as biological and diagnostic characteristics. Treatment literature has concentrated primarily on pharmacotherapy studies. Despite the lack of more varied treatment investigations involving depressed children, the current belief is that depression in children is similar to depression in adults (Reynolds and Coats 1986). Antidepressant medications such as Imipramine, Elavil, and Prozac are currently being used to target depressive symptoms in children, although the effectiveness of these medications is still being investigated.

The use of cognitive therapy with children and adolescents is a relatively new modality in the area of child psychotherapy, but research studies have demonstrated its effectiveness (Nissen 1986; DiGiusseppe 1981). Cognitive therapy can be particularly useful when treating children and adolescents with endogenous depressions.

Individual vs. Group Approach to Therapy

Many of the treatment studies with depressed adolescents show that cognitive therapy is an effective treatment modality; however, few current outcome studies with children have been published. Early findings suggest that individual therapy utilizing a cognitive approach is effective in treating children and adolescents who exhibit social skills deficits, poor peer relationships, limited problem-solving skills, low self-esteem and depressive symptoms (Birmaher, et al. 1996; Kaplan, et al. 1995). Unlike other individual therapeutic models, cognitive therapy involves a collaborative approach (child as active participant) that has been shown to be effective in engaging the child in treatment, thereby reducing the resistance that frequently occurs in the treatment of children and adolescents. Throughout the twelve-step protocol sessions, helpful suggestions in the form of clinical examples are provided to assist you in controlling the noncompliance that frequently occurs in the treatment of children and adolescents.

Although this manual has been designed primarily for use in individual therapeutic settings, it can easily be modified for group therapy. Various studies show that group treatment in general can be as effective, and in some studies, more effective, than individual treatment due to social facilitations, peer support, and peer feedback. Group therapy also provides the children with the opportunity to practice and role-play interpersonal behaviors and skills, while allowing them to see that they are not alone in having problems and conflicts (Reynolds and Coats 1986). Between the ages of six and twelve, most children are group oriented and are beginning to apply social rules learned in their previous stage of development. Children who are depressed, however, are deficient in social skills, and group therapy can provide the opportunity to develop positive interpersonal relationships, impulse control, and social skills; enhance self-esteem; and be more effective in problem solving and reality testing (Keepers 1987).

Throughout the twelve-step protocol, special notes provide suggestions for those clinicians interested in using this approach in group therapy settings. However, despite the effectiveness of utilizing cognitive therapy in group settings, the individual model therapy is more widely recognized in traditional mental health settings and clinics in the treatment of children and adolescents.

Facilitating Group Therapy

Group therapy is most effective with five to eight children per group. The group should meet once a week for ninety minutes. Prior to the first group therapy session, you should conduct individual interviews with prospective group members. Clinical evaluation of each child should be done utilizing appropriate assessment tools. Children must be adequately screened and prepared prior to joining a therapy group. Be sure to address any anxiety a child has about group therapy before the first group session.

Group rules and limits should be addressed in the first group session. While the children are encouraged to participate in the establishment of rules, you should set some basic ground rules. Feedback from the children regarding the rules is important. Please refer to the following suggestions:

o Encourage children to come on time.

o Emphasize that group will start and end on time even if only one child is present. When this occurs, children begin to learn and accept limits and boundaries.

o Arrange chairs in a circle, but not around a table. Nonverbal communication is an important group process because it involves the entire body.

o Do not allow interruptions when a participant is talking.

o Do not allow physical aggression or name-calling.

o Encourage each child to respect the group's privacy.

o Reinforce the importance of respecting one another's personal space.

o Discuss confidentiality issues.

o Discuss group's purpose, number of sessions, agenda issues, and what the children might get out of the group experience.

At the end of each group therapy session, encourage the children to share what they have just learned or experienced, and to discuss any problems or concerns. Also encourage the children to ask any questions they may have.

PART ONE

Theory
and
Treatment

CHAPTER ONE

An Introduction to Cognitive Therapy

The techniques in this book are based on the work from experts in the field of cognitive therapy, primarily Aaron T. Beck, who has worked extensively with adults exhibiting depressive symptoms. It is important for those of you who have minimal knowledge of cognitive therapy to familiarize yourselves with its key concepts as well as Beck's work.

Cognition, an essential concept of cognitive therapy, refers to what goes on in the mind. In more abstract terms, cognition is the psychological acquisition, processing, or organization and use of knowledge. Cognitions may be referred to as the thoughts, images, beliefs, underlying assumptions, or pictures that may be in your mind. How can this concept be utilized in therapy? What are the historical roots of this therapeutic process? Can cognitive therapy be effectively used in treating children? More importantly, is cognitive therapy an appropriate and useful treatment for childhood depression?

Briefly, cognitive therapy is a structured and systematic approach that focuses on the relationship between cognitions, emotions, and behavior. The most central feature of the theory is that the content of a person's thinking affects his or her mood. This idea is exemplified by the following exercise:

> Imagine that you're coming home from a long day at work. You're tired and you've just turned down a few offers to have dinner or attend the local happy hour. You have worked a long, grueling week. Although it is Friday, you decide to go home, throw a frozen dinner in the microwave, and take a snooze. You finally wake up after sleeping longer than you wanted and consider doing that basket of laundry you have been putting off for three weeks. After pondering over this laundry issue, you make the decision to do it (besides, who wants to do laundry on Saturday when the news is predicting 80 degree weather and above?). So . . . you gather up the clothes and make the long trek down (four floors) to the laundry room. Your apartment does not have an elevator. When you enter the

laundry room you are relieved that no one is using the washer or dryer. You think, "While they are out socializing at the local happy hour, I'll just zip through this laundry in about forty-five minutes." You load the washer, plug in your radio, and go about your business. About ten minutes later the lights go off, the washer stops, and, like everything else, your radio bites the dust. As you are standing there in silence and darkness, you hear a bump against the door. How do you feel? What do you think?

Typical Thoughts	Related Feelings
The landlord didn't pay the electric bill.	Angry
A fuse blew out.	Frustrated
There's a thunderstorm.	Afraid
Those wild neighborhood kids are playing a prank.	Angry

The following hypothetical situation illustrates how the cognitive model can be adapted to fit a younger population:

A group of thirty sixth graders arrives for homeroom. Their teacher, Ms. Miller, quickly urges them to sit down. She then informs them that their first-period class has been canceled due to an important announcement. She instructs the children to be on their best behavior because the principal will arrive shortly to discuss an important matter. After she finishes making this announcement, an alarm suddenly goes off in the building. The lights in the classroom begin to flicker. Ms. Miller runs to the door and looks quite startled. She then tells everyone in a loud voice to remain seated.

Typical Thoughts	Related Feelings
I'm getting suspended.	Angry
I failed the sixth grade.	Sad
A bomb is going to blow up the school.	Afraid
A famous performing artist is giving a free concert.	Happy
Teachers are going on strike.	Happy
Ms. Miller is retiring.	Sad

This exercise illustrates the relationship between feelings and thoughts. If you presented the second example to an audience of children, you would receive a variety of responses. However, while each child hears about the same situation, the way he or she perceives the situation will trigger different thoughts and feelings. In other words, the way a person feels is the result of his or her thoughts and perceptions; a person's thoughts about a situation are far more influential than the situation itself.

The historical development of cognitive therapy can be traced back to Albert Ellis, who developed *Rational Emotive Therapy* (RET) in 1955, after breaking away from his previous training and practice as a psychoanalyst. Ellis believed that human beings are born with a tendency to creatively invent certain, often unrealistic, ways of looking at themselves, others, and the universe. RET utilizes a comprehensive *thinking-feeling-acting* form of psychological treatment that relies upon the *ABC Theory of Irrational Thinking and Disturbance*. In RET, you look at the connection between *A*—the Activating event or experience; *B*—the individual's Belief system about what is occurring at *A*; and *C*—emotional or behavioral Consequences. RET stresses that *A* does not directly cause *C*, although it contributes to it. It is *B*, the intervening belief system about what is occurring at *A*, that more directly causes or creates *C*.

Ellis' therapeutic style was direct and confrontational. Other major schools of psychotherapy were opposed to Ellis' approach because he immediately and aggressively challenged the patient's irrational beliefs. They considered his method to be abrasive. Ellis' concept of making the patient aware of his or her emotional beliefs and the often inappropriate emotional consequences of those beliefs had a significant impact on the historical development of cognitive behavioral therapies.

The work of Aaron T. Beck followed up on Ellis' theory that events, thoughts, behaviors, and emotions are interrelated. Like Ellis, Beck was also a psychoanalytically trained therapist who reached the conclusion that the common psychological symptoms of depression are largely caused by cognitive overgeneralization and other forms of distorted thinking. He then constructed a highly cognitive form of therapy that parallels RET. Beck's version of cognitive therapy is an

> **active, directive** form of therapy; in essence, a time-limited, structured
> approach used to treat a variety of psychiatric disorders (i.e., depression,
> anxiety, phobias). It is based on an underlying theoretical rationale that an
> individual's affect and behavior are largely determined by the way in
> which he structures the world. His or her cognitions (verbal or pictorial
> events in his stream of consciousness) are based on attitudes or
> assumptions (schemas), developed from previous experiences (Beck 1979).

The basic assumption of cognitive therapy, according to Beck (1979), is that emotional disturbances, including depression, are caused by distortions in thinking on a conscious level. According to this theory, the disturbed, irrational, or distorted thinking of a depressed person includes three major elements—negative self-esteem, negative view of the past and present, and hopeless outlook for the future—that have been referred to as the *cognitive triad concept.*

As was indicated earlier, the main focus in cognitive therapy is on thoughts and cognitions. The cognitions a person has can strongly influence his or her emotions and behaviors. Cognitive therapy's major goal then is to correct a depressed person's distorted thinking by direct, rational, or logical examination of his or her views in order to help him or her gradually adopt a more realistic view of the self, the environment, and the future (Beck 1979).

Cognitive therapy has become the trend in verbal psychotherapy; however, it has been slow to catch on in treating children because few research studies have demonstrated the effectiveness of cognitive therapeutic techniques with children and adolescents.

As a mental health practitioner, you are probably aware that when children suffer from emotional or psychiatric disorders, treatment usually involves the entire family. In traditional family treatment, while the child is generally seen as the identified patient, he or she is often not actively involved in the treatment process. The child's active collaboration with the therapist, however, is an integral part of the cognitive therapy process. Also, it is important to note that when treating children with depression, parental treatment and family therapy may not be enough; individual treatment utilizing a cognitive behavioral approach may be warranted.

Good Self-Talk vs. Bad Self-Talk

A person's belief system is comprised of both rational and irrational beliefs. Children and adolescents, like adults, have a particular belief system. Rational beliefs are those that usually tend to be consistent with objective reality and lead to self-enhancing emotions and goal-directed behaviors. Irrational beliefs are generally distortions of reality, are expressed automatically, and lead to negative feelings that often block goal attainment. Irrational beliefs may also remain dormant or inactive and only be activated in specific situations or stressful events.

Although cognitive therapy has been defined and explained to some extent, I have yet to describe how this therapy process can be explained to children. To describe cognitive therapy as an action-oriented, directive verbal therapy in which the therapist challenges irrational beliefs and distorted thinking in an attempt to replace them with more rational, alternative ways of thinking may be appropriate for adults, but it is too abstract for children. In more concrete terms, cognitive therapy is a kind of "talking therapy" in which the therapist helps children spot negative ways of thinking or feeling during problem situations and teaches them the connection between thoughts and feelings. More specifically, children are taught that the emotions they feel are caused by the thoughts they are thinking. When children engage in *bad self-talk*, automatic negative thoughts and feelings, they may feel sad, angry, down in the dumps, or disappointed with themselves or the people around them. The therapist's major task is to help children challenge, or change, bad self-talk by using rational responses, or, in more concrete terms that children can understand—*good self-talk*. Good self-talk consists of words or statements children can say to themselves that will eliminate or decrease negative thoughts, beliefs, and feelings.

Some therapists may disapprove of using the words *bad* and *good* to illustrate the basic concepts of cognitive therapy. However, the terms bad self-talk and good self-talk are easily understood by children, particularly those who have limited cognitive abilities and who function intellectually within the low to average range. It has been determined that, starting from early childhood, children can acquire beliefs that are untrue and irrational about themselves and their surrounding world. These beliefs may then crystallize during later childhood and adolescence in response to school, family, peer pressure, or other interpersonal stressors.

The major objectives of therapy are

o relief of depressive symptoms

o prevention of the recurrence of depression by helping the child to identify and modify faulty thinking and dysfunctional behavior

o helping the child recognize and change cognitive structures leading to dysfunctional ideation and behavior

CHAPTER TWO

Affective Education and Cognitive Behavioral Interventions

Affective Education

Before you can teach a child how to modify negative ways of thinking and how thoughts influence emotions, you must first provide some *affective education,* and discuss the basic symptoms of depression. Affective education is a process in which the child learns how to identify feelings and emotions. After the child has demonstrated a basic understanding of feelings, the next procedure is to assist the child in recognizing the relationship between thoughts, feelings, and behaviors (Kendall 1991). Begin by asking the child to define depression in his or her own words. Children may explain depression by stating, "You know, depression" or "That's what my mom said." Some children will say, "I don't know," and others may accurately say, "I was sad and wanted to hurt myself." So you must educate them about the symptoms of depression by using a checklist, or any similar format in which they can identify the symptoms they recognize. Be sure to inform them that the primary feeling of depression is sadness or anger.

The next task involves educating the child about feelings. You may be surprised to learn that many children have difficulty verbalizing how they feel during problem situations. But most children are able to do so when provided with visual aids, or when feelings are demonstrated through role-playing. Through games, pictures, and role-playing, children are taught how to recognize feelings by becoming aware of what others look like when experiencing these emotions; recognition of behavioral cues that are associated with various emotions (such as, voice tone, facial expression, body gestures, and so on) is also emphasized. Keep in mind that the most important step taken in emotional problem solving is teaching the relationship between thoughts and feelings.

When I teach a child about feelings, I usually start the session by presenting a *feelings poster.* I inform the child that this poster may help him or her learn about and recognize different feelings, emphasizing that we can't see a feeling because a feeling is inside the person. However, the feelings of another individual can be identified by interpreting how the individual looks on the outside (facial expression, voice tone, physical reactions).

To make sure that your patient fully understands the concept of feelings, you might pose some questions to identify emotions. For example, if someone calls you a bad name, what do you do? How do you feel? Or if someone tells you that they like your new outfit, how do you feel?

For Group Therapy

In group therapy sessions, you can encourage the children to practice identifying, expressing, and acting out feelings. Distribute cards with different categories of feelings on them. Have some of the children make up a story about or act out the feeling and ask the others to guess the mood.

Cognitive Behavioral Interventions

The child is now ready to monitor his or her moods or feelings. I use three exercises that are described to the child as creative experiments, rather than homework assignments: "My Feeling Today Is," "Daily Mood Calendar," and "Mr. & Ms. Feel Good Daily Rating Sheet." These creative experiments help a child assess dominant moods during the day. The child can be taught to self-monitor moods, activities, thoughts, and pleasant events. However, monitoring mood is probably difficult for younger children due to their limited cognitive abilities.

When children make negative self-statements or engage in bad self-talk as a result of a problem situation, as the therapist, you must first help the child correct distortions of reality. Distortion is an important word but quite difficult to explain to a child. Basically, distortions may be referred to as "thinking errors," or faulty ways of perceiving situations. Here are some examples of how to define distortions to a child:

Ask if the child has ever spotted something silver shining brightly on the sidewalk and become excited, thinking he or she may have found a quarter, only to discover it is just a piece of aluminumn foil. The child's thinking was distorted—he or she assumed that the foil was a quarter but, in reality, it was just a piece of foil.

Ask if the child has ever seen a fuzzy picture on the TV. Explain to the child that when he or she feels depressed and has bad self-talk the experience is similar to a fuzzy TV picture. He or she doesn't see things clearly. So what does one do with a fuzzy TV picture? The screen must be fine-tuned and focused to clear up the picture.

By challenging the child's negative thoughts and distortions of reality, you are teaching the child to focus the TV screen in his or her mind and to see that the situation may not be as bad as initially expected.

The following case description may further clarify these concepts.

Ben is a twelve-year-old boy who was hospitalized for depressive symptoms and behavioral problems. He had very low self-esteem and referred to himself as being ugly, stupid, and an idiot. Although he exaggerated his deficits, Ben was not conventionally attractive and was being teased by peers about his looks. Ben assumed that he was disliked by everyone, including his parents, siblings, and peers at school. His mother reported that Ben was frequently involved in fights, many of which he initiated, and that he had few positive peer relationships. After one month of inpatient treatment that included cognitive therapy sessions, an antidepressant medication trial, and family therapy, his depressive symptoms had decreased significantly. The patient was quite popular in the hospital and had developed positive relationships with peers.

As Ben's discharge date approached, however, he began to engage in bad self-talk. He assumed that when he went back to school "everyone would beat him up and three hundred children would be on the playground, or on the school steps waiting to attack him." As Ben envisioned this attack, he made statements such as "I'm going to get beat up," "No one will like me," "I won't go to school," and so on; he experienced a setback.

Ben experienced feelings of sadness, anxiety, and fear. In just one session, in which his discharge was discussed, Ben reverted to a distorted reality. He experienced cognitive distortions based on distorted past experiences. Ben was never teased or beaten up by three hundred children. The therapist told him that he was having distortions, and using bad self-talk. Ben was familiar with this term because of examples he'd been given during previous sessions.

The primary goal of a therapist with this child, as with other children who engage in bad self-talk, is to teach that negative thoughts may lead to feelings such as sadness, fear, anxiety, anger, and so on.

Cognitive restructuring is an intervention that is used to challenge a child's bad self-talk, or cognitive distortion, and is often referred to as, "What's the Evidence" or "What If" (Stark 1991). These procedures are designed to modify the child's thinking and the premises, assumptions, and attitudes underlying his or her thoughts (Meichenbaum 1977). The child is taught to identify distorted thoughts, to evaluate the evidence for the thoughts, and to consider alternative interpretations. The child is also encouraged to think about what really would happen if the undesirable event occurred.

Here's how this procedure was utilized with Ben, who assumed that three hundred kids were going to beat him up when he got off the school bus. The therapist asked, "What is the evidence?" (Emery, et al. 1981). This involved working closely with Ben to find evidence that would support or refute his automatic negative thoughts, or bad self-talk and the underlying schemata:

Therapist: Okay, Ben, let me get this straight, three hundred children are going to beat you up when you go back to school?

Ben: I think so.

Therapist: Now, does this three hundred or so kids include the kindergarten kids and first and second graders?

Ben: No, I guess they are too little to want to beat me up.

Therapist: So, if you take away the kindergarten kids, the first and second graders, that leaves about how many kids who will be waiting to beat you up?

After a few probes and challenges like the one described in the dialogue above, the number of attacking children dwindled to about eighty seventh graders. The therapist then asked:

Therapist: Ben, do you think there will be about eighty seventh graders waiting to beat you up?

Ben: Yeah.

Therapist: What is your evidence?

Ben: I know everyone in my grade hates me and is going to tease me and beat me up.

Therapist: Do you know everyone in your grade?

Ben: Just about.

Therapist: Ben, have all of these kids, every one of them, teased and beaten you up before?

Ben: Well, not really.

Therapist: Ben, since eighty kids are not going to beat you up, name the kids who are going to be waiting for you at the school to beat you up.

Ben: (*pauses for a few minutes and responds*) Well, I know there will be fourteen or fifteen kids waiting to get me because my friend told me when I went home on a visit from the hospital.

At this point in the dialogue, the therapist finds an opportunity to change the focus for a bit and asks:

Therapist: You have a friend?

Ben: Yes.

Therapist: Is he in your grade?

Ben: Yes.

Therapist: (*challenging Ben*) I thought you didn't have any friends.

Ben: I have about three friends.

Therapist: What are their names?

Ben: Tommy, James, and Kenya.

Therapist: So you have three friends that will give you some support?

Ben: Yeah, they'll help me out I guess.

Therapist: Now let's get back to the fourteen or fifteen kids that still want to beat you up. Give me their names. This will help me get a better idea as to how many kids really want to fight you, okay?

Ben: Okay . . . uhmm . . . John, Earl, Jim . . . hmm . . . Let me see . . .

Therapist: Take your time, but so far you just identified three kids. You have about eleven or twelve left. Am I right?

Ben: I can't name them all.

Therapist: Think a little harder. Remember these are the kids that are after you.

Ben: John, Jim, Earl ... Oh, I forgot Tina.

Therapist: Okay, so John, Jim, Earl, and Tina. Anyone else?

Ben: No, I think just them. They are the ones who pick on me a lot and threaten to beat me up.

Therapist: So it looks like only about four kids may be after you when you return to school. Not fourteen or fifteen. Right?

Ben: Yeah.

Although Ben's fears and sadness subsided when he realized that at most, only four kids were after him, the therapist had to help him cope with the possibility of handling that stressful situation. Using the "What If" technique, the therapist helped Ben obtain a more realistic understanding of the meaning of the situation and to see that the probable outcome may not be so bad.

Refer to the following dialogue for further clarification of the "What If" technique:

Therapist: So what if four kids are going to be waiting to beat you up? What can you do?

Ben: I can always walk into the building with my friends.

Therapist: Okay, what if one of the kids walks over to you and starts to pick a fight or teases you? (Note: Ben was taught basic self-assertion skills through previous role-play enactments.)

Ben: (loudly) I'd say, get out of my face and leave me alone! I'm not taking your stuff any more!

Therapist: Good job. But what if the kid hits you?

Ben: (calmly states) I can take it; I've been hit before; I can always report it to the principal. I'll also ask my friends to come with me to help me explain what happened.

After "What's the Evidence" and "What If," depressed children should be taught to ask themselves, "Even if what I think turns out to be true, how bad is it?" (Emery, et al. 1981.)

The therapist used Beck's approach with Ben, which consisted of highly specific learning experiences designed to teach him to:

   o Identify and monitor negative, automatic thoughts (cognitions)

   o Recognize the connections between cognitions, affect, and behavior

   o Examine the evidence for and against distorted automatic thoughts

   o Substitute more reality-oriented interpretations for biased cognitions

   o Learn to identify and alter the dysfunctional beliefs that predispose him to distort his experiences (Beck 1979)

Cognitive behavioral techniques may also be used during therapy sessions with children. In cognitive therapy, these cognitive behavioral techniques involve the systematic alteration of the patient's ongoing behavior (Emery, et al. 1981).

Activity Scheduling

This involves planning pleasurable and goal-directed activities into the child's day (Stark 1991). Scheduling daily activities for a child helps to reduce boredom, passivity, and brooding. The process of activity scheduling should stress the importance of the child's active participation in the planning. You and the child may collaborate during a session to plan the child's schedule. Parents may also be actively involved in this process. It is important to note that "depressed children need to be gently, consistently, and persistently coaxed to participate in the scheduled activities" (Emery, et al. 1981).

Basic Social Skills Training

This should be incorporated into cognitive therapy sessions at some point. Social skills are an important part of the treatment of depression since most depressed children report social withdrawal and poor interpersonal relationships. Social skills exercises provide an opportunity to engage the depressed child in an action-oriented activity. Social skills training emphasizes basic assertiveness, eye contact, facial expression, appropriate voice tone, giving compliments, maintaining appropriate personal space, and so on. Teaching these social skills through role-playing will help build or enhance the skills. During sessions, you can provide the child with feedback as he or she practices these skills. The child can be given the creative experiment of practicing two social skills prior to the next session; these should be practiced when interacting with both peers and adults.

Cognitive Strategies

Children often have difficulty identifying thoughts during sessions, although they may be able to identify the stressful or problematic situation. During the session, you can encourage the child to imagine certain situations that may have bothered him or her during the week. While the child relives the situation through imagination, ask him or her to describe aloud any thoughts he or she may have while visualizing this situation. Role-playing the stressful situation with the child can also be helpful in identifying automatic thoughts (Stark 1991).

Self-Monitoring Thoughts. Children, like adults, should be encouraged to record thoughts between sessions, particularly when a change in mood is experienced. Self-monitoring has a number of functions: It is used as a procedure for increasing activity level and promoting restructuring. It serves as a method for directing a child's attention to more positive aspects, thus breaking the cycle of negative perceptions. It can help a child identify thoughts, feelings, events, activities, and situations. According to Stark:

> The self-monitoring of engagement in pleasant activities often leads to an
> increase in activity level, which leads to an improvement in mood, and
> consequently, more activity. It helps the child see that there are some
> positive things going on in his or her life (1991).

A child may be given exercises to record thoughts whenever they occur. When the child experiences changes in mood, the associated cognitions should be recorded as soon as possible. A child can write his or her thoughts in a journal or use the structured response column known as the "Dysfunctional Thought Record." I have modified this record in a variety of ways so that the child may have less difficulty understanding self-monitoring concepts. Examples are "Child Thought Record," "Joe's Spelling Test," "Daily Mood Log," "I Am Thinking," and "Enemy Camp vs. Enemy Destroyers." These exercises show the relationship between thoughts and feelings.

Self-Affirmation. A young child, or one who has difficulty replacing bad self-talk with good self-talk may respond well to self-affirmation (Emery, et al. 1981). This technique refers to replacing certain thoughts with other thoughts. The child is encouraged to repeat specific statements several times per day, particularly when feeling sad, angry, and so on. These statements may include, "I know my parents love me," "I like myself," "My looks are okay," "I can do it if I try," "I'm just as good as other kids," and so on. When these self-affirmation statements are repeated, self-esteem and positive feelings can be enhanced.

Coping Statements. These may also be referred to as good self-talk and are similar to self-affirmation statements in that they can be used to help a child respond adaptively to problem or stressful situations. For example, teaching the depressed child to say, "I tried my best" after taking an exam or to say, "Good job" after hitting a home run during the baseball game helps him or her to practice positive self-reinforcement, which in turn, will enhance self-esteem.

Relaxation Training. Relaxation techniques have been found to reduce symptoms of anger, anxiety, and low self-esteem. Because these are often associated with depressed mood, relaxation training is taught as a coping skill. It is important to first teach the child basic information about the relationship between stress, muscle tension, and depression. Then teach the child basic relaxation skills that emphasize the following:

o Choosing a quiet room

o Sitting or lying down quietly in a comfortable position

o Closing his or her eyes

o Choosing a positive word or phrase to repeat aloud or silently while exercises are practiced or thinking of a positive, relaxing scene

o Relaxing all muscles

o Breathing easy and naturally (As he or she breathes out, a favorite word or phrase should be repeated.)

o Continuing the exercise for fifteen to twenty minutes

Relaxation tapes may also be used once a child is taught basic muscle tension release exercises. You may want to make a tape with the child that he or she keeps and uses between the therapy sessions. Encourage the child to practice relaxation steps when faced with stressful situations that cause feelings of anxiety, anger, sadness, and so on.

In summary, keep in mind that the core of cognitive therapy treatment is to teach the child how to examine the validity of his or her beliefs and to teach strategies for subjecting these beliefs and thoughts to critical scrutiny. When the child learns how to identify his or her thoughts and learns how to record them, he or she should learn the three methods of challenging those thoughts:

1. Look at the evidence.

2. Explore alternative explanations and reasons.

3. "Even if what I think turns out to be true, how bad is it?" (Emery, et al. 1981).

The concepts and techniques presented in this manual are similar to cognitive therapy techniques that have been proven effective with adults. However, they have been modified to more appropriately meet the child's developmental needs. Generally, treatments for the depressed child have been limited to relaxation and social skills training; yet a depressed child exhibits many of the same cognitive features observed in adults with depression.

Cognitive therapeutic sessions with children, as with adults, should be well planned with specific guidelines so that the child can believe that he or she is capable of controlling his or her own behaviors and, therefore, of controlling his or her depressive symptoms. Social skills training should be emphasized during sessions so that the child can learn to cope with his or her daily life experiences. When you use cognitive-behavioral interventions, you should also emphasize during sessions that the child should practice those skills outside of the treatment sessions (Brown and Lewinsohn 1984). Role-playing may provide the child with the opportunity to generate alternative solutions to social problems that are relative to behavioral and emotional adjustment (Spivack, Platt, and Shure 1976; DiGiusseppe 1981).

In my experience as a clinical practitioner and psychologist, (working primarily with children and adolescents), it has become obvious that a child can communicate and verbalize his or her problems in an appropriate and insightful manner. This requires only a minimum of activities like therapeutic games or other play materials (dolls, clay, and so on). However, I am also aware that a very young child or one who is intellectually limited may require the use of play materials or games in order to express thoughts and feelings or discuss problem situations. It is important to consider the child's overall intellectual functioning or cognitive abilities before cognitive therapy can be successfully implemented.

CHAPTER THREE

Cognitive Therapy Course

The Course of Cognitive Therapy

This cognitive therapy course provides professionals with an easy-to-use format consisting of twelve sessions that may be spaced over a six- to twelve-week period, and is conducive to both individual and group therapeutic settings. Sessions may be held weekly or biweekly during this period. In addition, you will meet with the child twice prior to the first individual cognitive therapy session. These meetings should be used to establish rapport and to briefly educate the child about the basic concepts of cognitive therapy. During this period, you should assess the child fully for depression using familiar instruments. An initial assessment is done in order to obtain baseline data or general information regarding the child's clinical picture. In group therapy, prior to the first group session, conduct an assessment with each child to determine diagnostic profile and appropriateness for group therapy. I suggest the following assessment tools to obtain baseline measures or phenomenological descriptions of depression: K-SADS, Mini K-SADS, Child Depression Inventory, Beck Depression Inventory (can be used for children fourteen years of age and older), Piers Harris Self-Concept Scale.

You should assess the child using the same assessment tools or questionnaires at the end of each two-week period to measure progress toward treatment goals. These procedures should also be utilized to monitor the child's mood and symptoms throughout the duration of treatment. In collaboration with the child and his or her parents, develop a problem list (target symptoms), as well as a list of strengths, prior to the first scheduled cognitive therapy session.

During the course of cognitive therapy treatment, regularly scheduled meetings should be held with the child's parents in order to update them regarding their child's progress. Sessions with the parents should be held every two weeks or as otherwise determined by you. The parents are given the opportunity to ask questions and to exchange feedback. Educating the parents about the concepts and goals of cognitive therapy is an important element that will enhance the effectiveness of this treatment process.

Treatment Objectives

o Develop and enhance ability to identify feelings.

o Improve mood by decreasing depression.

o Eliminate suicidal ideation or behavior.

o Change aspects of one's negative thinking.

o Enhance self-esteem.

o Increase pleasant activities.

o Increase verbal communication skills.

o Develop appropriate problem-solving strategies.

o Develop and enhance social skills.

o Increase positive social interactions.

o Decrease anxiety and tension by learning how to relax.

Population

Children ages eight to fourteen, who exhibit depressive symptoms, and are within the average range of intellectual functioning are candidates for this type of therapy. For those therapists who prefer to use this manual with groups, three to four children in a group is recommended. When a co-therapy model is utilized, five to eight children should be involved in the group process. A time-limited cognitive group therapy for depression can be specifically applicable to children with primary depressive symptomatology. Most clinicians are in agreement that the cognitive therapy model has the flexibility to be utilized in either individual or group therapy sessions.

As previously stated, this manual has been developed as a result of adapting aspects from cognitive and behavioral theories of depression and from treatment programs designed specifically for use with adults (Lewinsohn 1978). It is primarily a semi-structured program, (designed to have flexibility based on the clinical needs of the child) utilizing a psychoeducational model with agendas, sessions, and rationale clearly defined, and the basic focus on teaching the depressed child effective ways of coping.

Common Terms

Agenda. This is a brief overview of what will occur in the session and is usually a collaborative effort when working with adults and older adolescents. However, children don't usually possess the cognitve abilities, motivation, or initiative to come up with an agenda. Prior to each session, the therapist should have an agenda prepared to review with the child at the beginning of the session. The child can be asked to provide any additional suggestions as well as provide any issues or concerns that may need to be addressed during the session. The following items may be included on the agenda for each session:

o Give the child the opportunity to discuss the week's events and report any changes in depressed mood (symptomatology).

o Discuss relationships between situations, moods, and cognition, and how the situation or activating event can influence or provoke a variety of emotional and cognitive reactions.

- Briefly review previous sessions, including the self-help assignments (creative experiments).

- Obtain the child's reaction to previous sessions.

- Introduce any new cognitive therapy technique or exercise.

- Teach and assign new creative experiments (such as homework, self-help assignments).

- Compile a summary of the current session.

- Record the child's reactions to the current session.

Presentation/Exercise ("Focus of Discussion"). The therapist educates the child by teaching new ideas or skills, often via the use of role-playing exercises, open discussion, or visual aids, and so on.

Feedback. The therapist encourages the child or adolescent to express views, perceptions, thoughts, and feelings about his or her experiences during the session. During group therapy sessions, participants are asked to share their concerns, feelings, and ideas with the other group members. Obtaining feedback from the child is important to be able to determine that the child understands the concepts introduced.

Creative Experiments. Commonly referred to as "homework," these are self-help assignments or therapeutic tasks to be completed by the child outside the clinical setting. For example, creative experiments may help the child monitor his or her mood and rate the degree of mastery and pleasure he or she experiences in relation to daily activities. They are also used to review and illustrate the main concepts learned during the sessions and to practice any new skill or activity. Creative experiments are important because they constitute the true application of the newly learned idea or skill. In essence, the major purpose of creative experiments is to supplement and reinforce the educational aspects of cognitive therapy. This procedure, according to Beck, "allows the therapist and the patient to review the previous week's activities at a glance, and it helps the therapist to relate the session to specific tasks, thereby avoiding side issues" (1979).

In this book, you are given a choice of creative experiments; each sheet has been drawn up with different pictures to account for gender and cultural diversity.

Noncompliance and Cognitive Therapy

Minimal information has been written on noncompliance and resistance in the treatment of children and adolescents; however, it is a common occurrence. It has been determined that the active, goal-oriented, here-and-now focus of cognitive therapy has been found to be effective with children (Wright and Schrodt 1987). The collaborative problem-solving approach helps to counter the difficulties that they have in working in a therapeutic relationship with an adult. You can immediately convey that you are not intending to convince or force the child into making particular choices, but instead intend to help develop new skills to evaluate current problems and current strategies of problem solving, as well as to begin working together as a team to identify possible alternatives to the child's current problems. Your major task is to teach the child new ways to evaluate his or her own thoughts, feelings, and behaviors. The process of cognitive therapy intends to bring automatic thoughts, or bad self-talk, and their underlying beliefs into full awareness, which in turn will help the child or adolescent gain an increased or heightened objective view of the events and situations he or she is experiencing. The cognitive therapy process will help the child be in better control of his or her thoughts, feelings, and behaviors. Issues focusing on control are often evident, especially for adolescents, therefore making the idea of the possibility of learning how to "gain" control of their lives an interesting and unusual prospect. The collaborative empirical working relationship helps to reduce oppositional and noncompliant behavior.

When working with a patient who is resistant to therapy, it is essential to reframe the presenting problem into a problem that the patient can relate to, thereby increasing the chance that he or she will see some value in coming to therapy to work on problems. Often the patient will not see the value of working on a problem that someone else has identified (parents, teachers).

Unlike most adults, a child usually does not have a clear idea or concept of what therapy is about. He or she may have misconceptions or stereotypes about therapy, such as, "Only crazy people go to see shrinks or head doctors. I am not crazy, so I am not going," or "I don't have any problems. My parents have the problems, not me." The child may also be resistant to the therapy, assuming that the therapist will share the perspective of the parents—the "all parents and adults stick together" syndrome. This misconception may subsequently lead the child to the conclusion that the therapist is "unsafe" to talk to because the therapist will be on the "parent's side."

It is also important to consider that unlike an adult, a child is usually being brought to therapy and is not coming of his or her own free will. Informing the child that the first session will be an "experiment" can be an effective and creative way of immediately communicating that the therapy process intends to be teamwork. You must communicate that the desires and opinions of the child are essential to the therapeutic process. This teamwork approach is an essential component of the cognitive therapy process that helps effectively deal with the problems of resistance to treatment.

The following dialogue is an example of a therapist dealing directly with a resistant child in their first meeting:

Therapist: How do you feel about being here today?

Child: I hate it! I don't want to be here. I don't know why my parents brought me in here. I don't know you and I'm not telling you one thing about me. There is nothing wrong with me, you should get my parents in here, they are the ones who are crazy, not me!

Therapist: Sounds to me like you are very angry about being brought in here to see me.

Child: Yeah, I'm angry, but I'm not crazy.

Therapist: So, does someone have to be "crazy" before coming to talk to a therapist?

Child: Why are you asking me? You should know that! You see crazy people all the time.

Therapist: Whoa, hold on a minute. You sure do have some strong opinions. But I must be honest with you, I don't believe that a person has to be "crazy" to come and talk to a therapist. I think therapy is a good place to come to talk to someone who is not going to take sides with anyone and who will work with you to work out whatever problems or concerns you have. I help a lot of children and teenagers learn how to overcome a variety of problems. Sometimes, two heads are better than one. What do you think of that?

Child: Yeah, two heads can be better than one, but the two heads have to be able to trust each other. I don't even know you.

Therapist: Your point is well taken. You don't know me, but we will get to know each other. I also agree with you 100 percent about the importance of being able to trust each other. I wouldn't recommend just trusting anyone. Also, it isn't real easy to start trusting someone you just met. Right?

Child: Yeah. Especially someone who's probably going to agree with everything my parents say.

Therapist: Do you think I'll do that?

Child: Probably.

Therapist: Actually, I appreciate your honesty. Most teenagers who first come here feel the same way until they get a better idea of what this type of therapy is all about. Have you ever gone to therapy before?

Child: No.

Therapist: Okay. Well maybe we could talk for a minute about what therapy is and isn't. Then, maybe you'll have a better idea about what goes on at a place like this. Okay?

Child: Yeah, I guess so.

Therapist: Well, many of the teenagers that I have seen at one time or another begin to have trouble coping with family difficulties. It's often frustrating for the teenager to be treated like a kid at times, yet at other times be expected to act and behave like an adult. It can be a very confusing time at home and sometimes even a confusing time with friends and in school. Sometimes all this frustration builds up to make a lot of anger and confusion in your life. Coming to therapy often helps teenagers learn new ways to gain control of what feels like a very out-of-control time. Do you ever feel frustrated with how things are going for you?

Child: You know it. I feel very frustrated. But I can handle things on my own. I don't really have any big problems.

Therapist: Okay, problems don't have to be huge or big. Actually, it's not a bad idea to try and deal with problems while they are small. Something does seem to be going on for you that has really upset you. Why do you think your parents brought you here today?

Child: My parents like to blame me for all their problems. Really, I think they are the ones having problems. They are mad at me because I have been fighting with them. They just want me to do everything they say and do it at the exact second they say it. I'm not a robot. They make me so mad, they are always on my case. They say one thing and do another. My mom is famous for saying, "Don't do as I do, do as I say." But I'm sure you'll agree with them and take their side of the story.

Therapist: I can tell you now that I won't be taking "sides." I would really rather hear your side of the story. Okay?

Child: Well . . . Okay. But I'm not coming back. I don't need this.

Therapist: Okay, you don't have to make any promises. Let's just handle today sort of like an experiment. At the end of our meeting, we can decide whether to continue the experiment.

Child: Okay, but what do you mean by "experiment"?

Therapist: I mean, let's experiment with whether or not we think we can get to know each other and whether it seems like we would make a good team. Remember the idea of "sometimes two heads are better than one"? . . . Let's check it out.

Child: Alright.

Therapist: Okay. Let's get back to you. Why don't you go ahead and fill me in on your side of the story.

Child: Well, it's like this: My mom and dad have been. . . .

As you can see from the above dialogue, this therapist will work to continue the process of diminishing the resistance of this child (in this case, a teenager). At no point in the dialogue did the therapist force the teen to talk. Instead, the therapist focused on providing choices to the adolescent, while not appearing annoyed or intimidated by the angry responses. Dealing openly and honestly with the resistance is the best strategy for attempting to overcome the resistance and begin forming a therapeutic alliance.

PART TWO

The Twelve-Session
Treatment Curriculum

The following sections consists of twelve protocol sessions. You may modify sessions based on the particular needs of each child, or you may choose to only use portions of the manual for therapeutic purposes.

CHAPTER FOUR

Session I:
Depression and Feelings Identification

Objective: To familiarize the child with the concepts of depression, cognitive therapy, and feelings

Introduction

Engage the child using a warm-up game or other age-appropriate activity.

Agenda

- o Discuss the child's therapy expectations.
- o Define depression and feelings identification.
- o Address specific issues or concerns identified by the child.

Presentation/Exercise

Expectations. Briefly discuss cognitive therapy as a method of individual treatment and the role of the therapist, as well as the child's perception of his or her own involvement in treatment (why he or she is coming to therapy; reason for referral, hospitalization, and so on). Encourage the child to identify the problem (in his or her own language) which brought him or her into treatment.

For Group Therapy

In group settings, the Get Acquainted Name Game, or other introductory break-the-ice technique, may be used as a warm-up exercise so children who are not familiar with each other may introduce themselves. The game often relieves feelings of anger and tension, as well as creates a fun and relaxing environment for the first session:

Instruct the children to think about something they like that begins with the first letter of their first name. Give the following examples: "My name is Pam and I like pizza. My name is Charles and I like cats." Then ask for a volunteer to go first. After the child states his or her name and what he or she likes, the next child has to remember the name of the child who went first as well as what the child likes before he or she is given a chance to share his or her own example. The exercise becomes more enjoyable as the children take their turns and attempt to recall the other group participants' names and what they like.

Definition of Depression. The session begins when you first pose the question, "What is depression?" to the child. Encourage the child to give explanations regarding his or her perception of depression as well as thoughts and feelings associated with it (sad, lonely). In other words, try to elicit the child's view or understanding of depression.

You should be familiar with the symptomatology of depression. The *Diagnostic and Statistical Manual of Mental Disorders* (*DSM-IV*) is a valuable resource for describing the clinical course of depressive illness (see "Dysthymia and Major Depressive Episode" in the *DSM-IV* for further clarification).

Define depression and review the following depressive symptoms. Primary symptoms can be written on a chart or chalkboard.

Symptoms. Sad, blue, hopeless, down, bored, irritable, cranky, tearful, poor concentration (i.e., inability to complete school assignments), low self-esteem, suicidal ideation, sleep disturbances, appetite disturbances (decrease or increase), poor peer relationships, guilt feelings, somatic complaints (i.e., headaches, stomachaches), psychomotor agitation (i.e., fidgetiness, restlessness).

Note: Be aware that depression manifested in children may look different than depression in adults. Children may not describe themselves as being sad, down in the dumps, or irritable, although these symptoms can be seen, perhaps, in a persistent sad facial expression. A child may continue to show interest and engage in activities; however, he or she may exhibit symptoms of apathy and boredom. Acting out and showing other behavioral problems in the home and school environments, as well as appetite changes that lead to weight loss or gain, may be other signs of childhood depression. Deterioration in academic performance and changes in a child's normal personality (an energetic, talkative child may become lethargic, quiet, and withdrawn) may constitute depressive illness.

At the beginning of each new session, summarize concepts addressed in previous sessions; all subsequent sessions will begin with a short summary of the session format and the theme of the previous session.

Feelings Identification and Socialization to the Cognitive Therapy Model

The following examples will serve as illustrations to help you define and explain the cognitive behavioral approach to both a child and an adolescent.

The therapist has greeted ten-year-old Johnny, and they have gone through the initial rapport-building stage. The therapist begins to elicit information from Johnny regarding his understanding of being brought in for treatment:

Therapist: So, Johnny, do you know why your mom brought you in to see me today?

Johnny: I'm not sure, I think she's worried about me.

Therapist: What's going on that you think your mom might be worried about?

Johnny: I don't know.

Therapist: Well, sometimes it's hard for kids to describe or talk about things they're not sure about, but you're right, your mom has been feeling a little worried about you. She told me that you've been feeling kind of down. Do you know what feeling down means?

Johnny: Yeah, it means not too good.

Therapist: You're right. Oftentimes, kids your age begin to feel down, sad, blue, or not too good about themselves. Maybe things are not going too good for them at school or at home and they start to have sad feelings. Sometimes kids become irritable—you know, cranky or angry. Do you ever have these feelings?

Johnny: Sometimes. Like when my mom asks me to do stupid things like pick up my clothes, I get mad and tell her that I don't feel like it.

Therapist: And what happens next?

Johnny: My mom gets real mad and starts to yell. She yells at me all the time.

Therapist: When your mom yells, how do you feel?

Johnny: I feel angry. She doesn't yell at my brother.

Therapist: How old is your brother?

Johnny: Four.

Therapist: I see. Johnny, since your brother is younger than you are, maybe your mom doesn't expect as much from him. She probably sees you as the big brother and expects a little more from you and you might not think this is fair. What do you think?

Johnny: I think she picks on me for no reason and I feel mad. Sometimes I think she doesn't like me and likes my brother more.

Therapist: Johnny, I talk with a lot of kids your age that feel angry, sad, or mad when things don't go well for them. My job as a therapist is to help kids feel better about themselves and to feel better about what is going on in their lives. In order for me to help kids learn about their feelings, I use the "Mr./Ms. Feel Good Daily Rating Sheet" (see chapter 7) (*therapist shows Johnny the sheet*). Johnny, you mentioned earlier that you sometimes feel mad, angry, and sad. Look at the scale on this sheet. It goes from one to ten. One means that you don't feel sad at all, and ten means that you are very sad or depressed. Children who often feel sad, angry, or down may be depressed. You'll learn a lot about your feelings and what depression is by coming in to see me. I'll teach you ways to change the way you think when you are feeling sad or mad. Before I talk to you about depression, let's look at this scale. On this scale, where do you think you would be? Remember, one means that you are not feeling sad or depressed, or even cranky or mad, and ten means that you are feeling very sad or depressed, or mad.

Johnny: That picture shows the girl looking very happy.

Therapist: Yeah. She does look happy. But how do *you* feel on a scale of one to ten?

Johnny: I don't know.

Therapist: A ten can mean that you feel very sad, depressed, and down. Do you ever feel like a ten?

Johnny: Sometimes, but not always.

Therapist: Tell me the number on the scale that best fits how you have felt during the past week.

Johnny: I think a seven.

Therapist: The number seven tells me that you are probably having more sad feelings than happy ones. One way I can help children like yourself feel better—not sad or depressed or angry—is to teach you how your thoughts can make you feel bad inside. Sometimes children as well as adults have thoughts that get mixed up. These thoughts can cause you to feel bad. In order to help you feel better about yourself, I will be doing cognitive therapy with you.

Johnny: What's that?

Therapist: Cognitive therapy is a grown-up word and somewhat hard to explain to children, but I'll do my best. Cognitive therapy is a type of talking therapy. When your mom brings you here to see me, we'll be talking together. This talking therapy can help you see when you are having bad thoughts or talking badly about yourself. These negative thoughts can make you feel depressed, angry, or sad. When kids talk badly about themselves or think about themselves and others in a negative way, this is called bad self-talk. My job is to help you change your bad self-talk by helping you use good self talk. When you get rid of the bad self-talk, you'll start to feel better. Good self-talk uses words that will help stop bad self-talk.

The therapist will most likely change his or her presentation when explaining cognitive therapy to an adolescent.

The therapist has greeted fourteen-year-old Cindy, and they have gone through the initial rapport-building stage. The therapist begins by asking Cindy about some of the problems she is currently experiencing and what her understanding is of why her parents brought her to therapy:

Cindy: I don't know why my parents want me to come here, there is nothing wrong with me. It's not like I'm crazy or something. I just can't stand my parents; they're ruining my life!

Therapist: How are they ruining your life?

Cindy: They are constantly screaming and yelling at me. They hate all my friends and won't let me go anywhere. They are always on my back. They refuse to let me go out with boys. They are so old-fashioned. If they get their way, I'll have no friends at all.

Therapist: It sounds like you think your parents are too tough on you and that they have too many restrictions. It must be hard trying to make friends and be liked, yet still try to follow your parents' rules and expectations.

Cindy: Yeah, it's real tough. My friends don't have so many rules and restrictions to follow. My two best friends have boyfriends and they're only fourteen years old.

Therapist: Cindy, I work with a lot of teenagers who are having problems at home. I would like to help by working together with you to learn new ways of thinking and solving problems; this is called cognitive therapy. Cognitive therapy is a type of talking therapy. You and I put our heads together to explore how your thinking patterns may be affecting how you feel and behave.

Cindy: That sounds okay, but how can coming to see you change how my parents treat me? They are never this strict with my brother. He gets away with practically everything. Not me!

Therapist: Well, that's a good question. Basically, by us working together, we can focus on you developing new ways to get what you want. What have you done up until now to try and get what you want from your parents?

Cindy: I don't know ... fighting and yelling at them ... telling them off.

Therapist: Okay, those are certainly ways of expressing yourself. Do these strategies work? Do you get what you want?

Cindy: No. It makes things worse. They get more angry with me. Nothing works!

Therapist: You're right, Cindy, none of those strategies have worked; however, you and I can work together to develop new negotiation strategies that will help you get along better with your family. Also, sometimes teenagers are feeling down, depressed, angry, or irritable, which can complicate the problem. This type of therapy will help you recognize what role your thoughts play in how you are feeling and behaving. You will be learning about bad and good self-talk. When teenagers like yourself talk about themselves and their problems in a negative manner, this negative talk can be referred to as bad self-talk. Cognitive therapy will help you replace or substitute your negative talk or negative thoughts with good self-talk. Do you understand how this therapy may help you begin to work out things at home?

Cindy: I guess, but it probably won't work.

Therapist: How about giving it a try first?

Cindy: Okay.

Once the child has been socialized to the cognitive therapy model, you can begin the process of helping the child learn to identify feelings by presenting the "Feelings Poster." You may then state, "This chart will help you identify different feelings or emotions." Review each feeling on the chart in a concrete, age-appropriate manner. Encourage the child to identify various feelings based on the pictures. Remember the following points during the session:

o Emphasize that we can't see a feeling; a feeling is inside the person. However, we may be able to determine the feelings of another individual based on how the person looks on the outside by interpreting facial expression, voice tone, physical reactions, and so on.

o Give the child additional feedback or praise for emphasizing specific nonverbal expressive clues, such as facial expressions, posture, and gestures. Then summarize these points by asking the child, "How can we tell how someone is feeling?" Answers should include:

1. By looking at the facial expressions and actions

2. By listening to what the person says or how they say it

3. By asking, "How do you feel?" (Weissberg and Gesten 1980)

Coping Skills

How does the child deal with problems? Assess the child's coping skills by providing examples, such as, "If someone calls you a bad name . . ." Ask the child how he or she would handle the situation. Would the child yell, scream, have temper tantrums, fight, cry, or express suicidal ideations or threats? Encourage the child to identify other problematic situations in which feelings or emotions may arise.

Feelings/Coping Exercise

Provide examples of interpersonal situations that can be put on index cards and that may evoke a variety of feelings. They can include the following:

o When someone tells me that they like my new outfit, I feel . . .

o When someone pushes past me and steps on my foot, I feel . . .

o When my older brother doesn't help me with my homework, I feel . . .

Then review the child's responses to these situations. Also, encourage the child to share similar experiences relative to the above examples.

Role-Playing Feelings. During the session, encourage the child to practice expressing his or her own feelings. Then distribute cards with the names of various feelings printed on them. Instruct the child to choose a card and make up a story about the feeling. The child will most likely feel more comfortable with this exercise if you also take a card and create a story.

You and the child can also engage in a role-play enactment where one person has to guess the feeling that is being portrayed. After the feeling is identified, the child then makes up a story about the feeling. Take turns dividing cards and demonstrating feelings depicted on the card. Some feelings to act out include happiness, sadness, fear, or anger. This creative task can also be done in group therapy sessions.

For Group Therapy

In group therapy sessions, encourage each child to practice expressing a variety of feelings. The Feelings Poster can be used to elicit identification of feelings from group participants. Then distribute index cards with the names of different feelings and emotions printed on them. Ask the children to break into two or three small groups, depending on the number of participants, and make up a group story about the feeling written on the card. After doing so, ask the children to act out the story, emphasizing the particular feeling or emotion written on the card. The remaining one or two groups are asked to guess the feeling that was acted out by the participants. Each group takes a turn.

Feedback

Try to elicit thoughts and feelings from the child about today's session in order to get the child's overall perception of his or her experience.

Creative Experiment (Homework)

First, explain what a creative experiment is. Then hand out the experiment "My Feeling Today Is ..."

Note: This exercise may not be suitable for an adolescent. As a substitute creative experiment, the older child should keep a brief diary or log in which he or she reports primary feelings experienced during the day. The creative experiment "My Thoughts for Today" (see chapter 7) can also be utilized.

As stated in chapter 3, creative experiments are commonly referred to as homework, self-help assignments, or therapeutic tasks to be completed by the child outside the clinical setting. Since this is the first session in which the creative experiment is utilized, you may want to refer to the following example to demonstrate how to explain this important concept to a child:

Therapist: After each session I am going to give you an assignment, or task, that I call a creative experiment, to do at home. This experiment will help you remember what we talked about during our session. A creative experiment is helpful because you will practice things that you have learned about. Creative experiment is a funny term, huh?

Johnny: Yeah. Why is it called a creative experiment?

Therapist: A creative experiment is similar to a homework assignment that you get from your teacher at school. But a creative experiment is different, and you won't get a grade on it. A creative experiment can be fun and interesting because you'll be doing something new and different. When you are finished with the creative experiment, you'll bring it in for me to look at, just like you would creative experiment, you'll bring it in for me to look at, just like you would do for school. I also think of creative experiments as being like special projects that will help me see what you've learned about yourself, your feelings, and your thoughts. Okay?

Johnny: Okay.

Parents of younger children (twelve and under) are encouraged to monitor the completion of the experiments as they would do with normal schoolwork. However, therapists who work primarily with adolescents will often encounter resistance and noncompliance with the completion of creative experiments. If resistance occurs during the course of treatment, it is important for you to continue to provide the adolescent with homework assignments and review them during the session. When the adolescent fails to bring in the homework, it becomes your responsibility to review this during the session. Try to explore with the adolescent his or her noncompliance regarding the completion of these tasks. It is important to make sure that you educate the adolescent regarding the purpose of creative experiments.

Possible Reasons for Noncompliance with Homework Assignments:

o Child did not fully understand the homework assignment. You did not adequately demonstrate the specific technique or exercise during the session.

o Child does not see the value or point of the assignment.

o Child does not agree with the treatment goals.

o Child may feel coerced or pressured to complete assignments.

o Child may perceive the expectations for completing the homework as demanding or idealistic ("impossible").

o Noncompliance with homework could be further indication that the general issue of resistance to treatment was not adequately resolved in the beginning stages of treatment.

Feelings Poster

HAPPY

ANGRY

SAD

SURPRISED

AFRAID

ANXIOUS

TIRED

BORED

My Feeling Today Is...

Name_____   **Date**_____

Directions: Draw in the expression
that best describes your
current feeling.

HAPPY   **SAD**   **ANGRY**   **AFRAID**

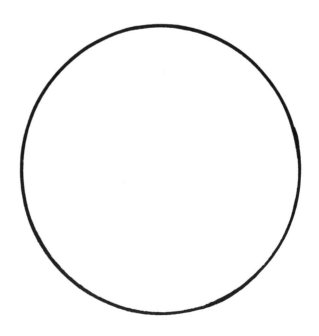

CHAPTER FIVE

Session II: "Why Me? The Story of Evan" or "What's Wrong, Jenna?"

Objective: To help the child realize that he or she is not alone by identifying problematic situations of others

Introduction

Conduct a brief review of last session, including depressive symptoms and creative experiment. Encourage the child to discuss his or her reactions to the previous session.

Agenda

- Review the concept of feelings.

- Introduce either "Mr./Ms. Feel Good," "Why Me? The Story of Evan" or "What's Wrong, Jenna?"

- Deal with specific issues or concerns identified by the child.

Presentation/Exercises

Review the "Feelings Poster" and ask the child to identify primary emotions such as anger, happiness, sadness, fear, and so on. The primary emotion for depression is sadness; however, in children, irritability is frequently experienced as well, and is often the dominant symptom.

Present "Why Me? The Story of Evan," or for older children "What's Wrong, Jenna?" Encourage the child to read the story. If the child has difficulty, you should read the story aloud. Generate appropriate questions concerning the character's behavior, thoughts, and feelings. The child should be able to identify feelings in the story, and also be able to verbalize his or her reactions and thoughts. Ask the child to relate Evan's or Jenna's experiences to his or her own life situation. Differences, as well as similarities, should be addressed during the session.

For Group Therapy

Instruct the group members to read the appropriate story and look for symptoms of depression and examples of feelings. Conduct a group discussion in which you elicit from the children their personal situations in which they experienced similar feelings as those described in the stories.

Feedback

Try to elicit from the child his or her thoughts and feelings about today's session.

Creative Experiment

Hand out and explain the "How I Feel Sentence Completion Worksheet." At the end of the session, give the child the "Daily Mood Calendar." This calendar is to be reviewed with the child and posted in an accessible area in the home environment. The child is expected to complete the calendar at the end of each day.

How I Feel
Sentence Completion
Worksheet

Name_____   Date_____

1. The worst thing I could do is_____.

2. The best thing I could do is_____.

3. The worst thing that a friend could do is_____

_____.

4. The best thing that a friend could do is_____

_____.

5. The best thing that a parent could do is_____

_____.

6. The worst thing that a parent could do is_____

_____.

7. The best thing that a sibling (i.e., brother/sister) could do

is_____.

8. The worst thing that a sibling (i.e., brother/sister) could

do is_____.

9. I usually feel _____.

10. Today I feel _____.

Daily Mood Calendar

Name_____   Month_____

> Color in the square using a color that best describes
> your overall mood each day. Key: Blue = Sad; Red =
> Angry; Yellow = Happy; Green = Neutral/Fair

Week 1   Date_____To_____

Sunday	Monday	Tuesday	Wednesday	Thursday	Friday	Saturday

Week 2   Date_____To_____

Sunday	Monday	Tuesday	Wednesday	Thursday	Friday	Saturday

Week 3   Date_____To_____

Sunday	Monday	Tuesday	Wednesday	Thursday	Friday	Saturday

Week 4   Date_____To_____

Sunday	Monday	Tuesday	Wednesday	Thursday	Friday	Saturday

Why Me?   The Story of Evan

By

Charma D. Dudley, Ph.D.

Illustrated by

David Turner

Evan is a ten-year-old boy who lives at home with his mother, brother, and sister. He recently started fifth grade.

Evan doesn't have a best friend and he rarely plays with anyone. Most of the time he plays by himself and feels lonely. At school, he usually sits alone, watching the other kids play. When other kids ask him to play dodge-ball or soccer, he shakes his head, "No." Evan thinks, "I can't play sports. I'm not any good, and the kids

don't like me anyway." Evan remembers a day
when he tried to kick a ball; he fell flat on his
back, and everyone laughed at him. Evan was
very embarrassed and felt sad. He thought, "I'm
a jerk; everyone thinks I'm stupid and clumsy.
They'll never ask me to play again, and if they
do, I'll say no, because they'll just tease me again
and laugh."

Things aren't any better for Evan at home. He is always arguing with his brother, Trevor, and sister, Chelsea, because they pick on him and call him goofy names. Evan thinks they treat him unfairly. Sometimes Evan tells them to shut up or yells at them. When he is feeling angry he goes to his room. It seems easier to shut the door, and "besides," he thinks, "no one cares about me anyway." He feels that everybody picks on him - the kids at school, even his own brother and sister.

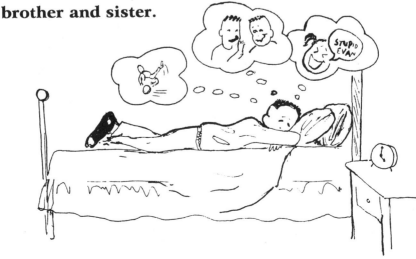

"Maybe it's the way I look," Evan thinks. "I wish I was different. Mom doesn't understand me either. She's just too strict. She has too many rules and chores. 'Clean up your room, Evan, take out the garbage.' She expects me to do everything - NAG, NAG, NAG and she lets Chelsea and Trevor get away with murder. They don't do any chores, but she's always hard on me. She never says nice things to me. She just yells. And, when things go wrong, I'm always blamed!"

"What is wrong with me?" Evan thinks. "I have no friends, my own brother and sister don't play with me. My mom pays no attention to me. Sometimes I feel so bad I wish I could disappear, then everyone would forget me. I'm just stupid, ugly, and a nerd." Evan often feels angry inside and cries when he is alone.

When people like Ms. Jones, Evan's fifth
grade teacher at school, ask him what is wrong,
he lies and says, "Nothing," because he thinks no
one really cares. Evan doesn't know how to
express his feelings and believes that "people
don't understand me anyway." When he feels
like this, he goes to his room and sometimes
goes to sleep. At least when he sleeps, "all
problems go away."

Evan has thought about hurting himself many times. He even knows how he'd do it. He believes that would take all of his problems away.

Today his short period of sleep is interrupted by a knock on his bedroom door. "Evan, are you okay?" his mother asks as she enters his room. Evan answers in a muffled voice, "I'm okay," as he attempts to hold back his tears. "Evan, I have been worried about you. You didn't come to dinner when I called you a few minutes ago. Please tell me if you need to

talk with me about something." Evan shakes his head no. "I'm...I'm okay," he stammers. Evan's mother has noticed that he has been acting differently during the past few weeks.

She has tried to talk to him on several occasions, and Evan has refused to open up. "Evan has been going to his room a lot and avoiding conversations with me, his brother, and sister. He's also been very cranky and more sensitive than usual," his mother thinks.

"Evan, honey, we need to talk. I know that something has been bothering you. I have been worrying about you lately," his mother states. Evan turns away from his mother, not wanting her to see the tears falling down his face. "You can't help me, no one can. You don't understand," Evan sadly states.

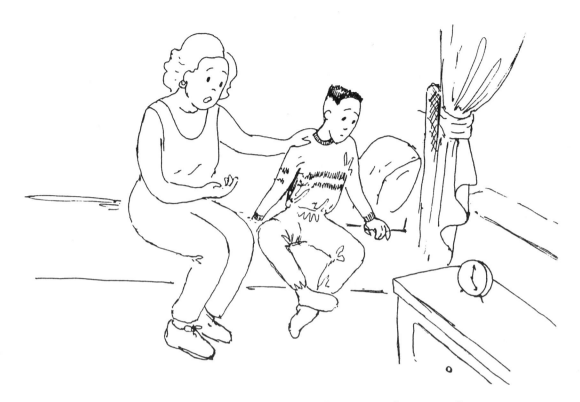

Evan's mother moves closer to him and puts her arms around him. "You may be right, Evan, I know you are hurting right now, but I don't know why," she explains as she tries to comfort him. Evan's mother continues to gently question him about his behavior, hoping that he will begin to open up.

Evan finally blurts out, "No one likes me, I have no friends, I wish I wasn't around anymore." Evan's mother is surprised by his outburst and is even more concerned about his statements. She has heard that children Evan's age can become depressed. "Evan, do you feel sad?" she asks. Evan answers, "Yes, all the time, and I feel mad too." "Is anything going on at school?" his mother asks. "Why do you and Ms. Jones keep asking me questions? Just leave me alone," he angrily states as he runs from the room.

Evan's angry response prompts his mother to contact his teacher the next day at school. After talking with Ms. Jones, Evan's mother is advised that he should receive counseling. Ms. Jones also informs her that within two weeks, she and the school counselor will be conducting group sessions that focus on self-esteem issues. She also tells Evan's mother that he may be depressed.

"Tomorrow, the school counselor and I will

be meeting with those children who would
benefit from these sessions. I will make sure
that Evan is put on the list. In the meantime,
I'll schedule an appointment for him to see the
school counselor," Ms. Jones states. Evan's
mother breathes a sigh of relief and thanks Ms.
Jones. "Don't worry," she reassures Evan's
mother, "Evan will get the support he needs."

Ms. Jones later pulls Evan aside after class
and tells him about the new group. "Tomorrow,
the school counselor and I will meet with you
and a few other kids to give you more
information about what we will be talking
about. This group will help you see that other

kids may be having feelings similar to yours. Just talking and listening to each other will make you feel better and not all alone. So what do you think, Evan?" "I'll give it a try," Evan states as he walks away.

The next day as Evan sits in his first group session and listens attentively to Ms. Jones and the school counselor, he thinks, "Other kids also feel this way. Wow!! People do care."

What's Wrong, Jenna?

By

Charma D. Dudley, Ph.D.

Illustrated by

David Turner

Jenna is a fourteen-year-old girl who lives at home with her mother and seventeen-year-old brother. Jenna's parents were divorced two years ago. After the divorce, Jenna's father left their hometown to take on a job in a big city over two hundred miles away. Jenna occasionally sees her father on weekends and misses him very much.

Sometimes she feels angry that her parents divorced, although she remembers the arguments her parents frequently had. Over the past year, Jenna has felt cranky and sad, preferring to be left alone. She also has had difficulty falling asleep and often worries that her father no longer loves her.

A couple of days ago, she got into a
shouting match with her best friend, Tanya,
when she jokingly called Jenna a know-it-all for
getting an A on her English test. Jenna accused
her friend of being jealous and told her that she
needed to study harder. Jenna thought, "Tanya
doesn't realize how hard I had to study for this
test, since I haven't been able to concentrate
lately." Tanya then called Jenna "a dork, with a
capital D." A couple of their friends joined in
the teasing and Jenna could feel her blood start
to boil. Jenna thought to herself, "What's wrong
with me, why do I feel so angry?" Instead of
apologizing to her friend and admitting that she

was being too sensitive for getting upset over something as stupid as an English test, Jenna called her friend stupid, and some other choice words, and angrily walked away.

Jenna was in a hurry to get to gym class where tryouts were being held for junior varsity cheerleading, pom-pom girls, and majorettes. Jenna and Tanya had made a pact to try out together for the cheerleading squad since they were both cheerleaders at their junior high. Jenna had been considering trying out for the pom-pom team since they frequently did somersaults, as well as dance steps in their routines.

When she entered the gym class, over one hundred girls were standing around talking about the tryouts. Some were in the same situation as Jenna and were not certain what squad they were interested in. As Jenna was thinking about her decision, she noticed that Tanya, who had entered the gym with a group of girls that Jenna didn't know very well, completely ignored her. Jenna became very upset. She could feel her face getting hot. "So she's mad at me. I'm the one who should be mad, she was the one calling me a dork and making fun of my A. She has a lot of nerve walking past me and ignoring me. Some best friend." Jenna thought to herself, "I should go right over there and give her a piece of my mind."

This thought was interrupted when another girl, named Shari, asked Jenna if she was trying out for the pom-pom squad. Jenna stated that she had been planning to try out for the cheerleading squad. Shari seemed surprised and said, "You're such a good dancer. I've seen your moves." Jenna smiled and really liked the positive comments she received from Shari, although she did not think she was such a good dancer. Jenna said, "Thank you, Shari, I do like to dance, but I don't think I'm good enough to be on the pom-pom squad."

As Shari talked on and on about the pom-pom squad, Jenna began to think, "Maybe I should do this instead of cheerleading; I like to dance." She also began thinking about all the new dance steps she had learned from watching videos and the teen dance programs on television. While alone in her room at home, Jenna would frequently practice the dances she learned from television. However, no one knew that she danced in front of her mirror, not even Tanya.

Well, almost no one knew. Jenna was harassed and teased by her brother several months ago. He had glimpsed her practicing and loudly mocked her. "Trying to dance, trying to dance," he shouted throughout the house. After that incident, Jenna made sure that she locked her door when she practiced her routines.

Jenna was brought out of her dreamworld when Shari asked, "So what are you going to do, cheerleading or pom-poms?" adding, "It would be nice if we could try out together." Jenna hesitated for a moment, but said, "Yeah, I'll try out" after she stole a quick glance at her so-called best friend, who was practicing cartwheels with the other girls. Jenna thought, "She doesn't even know that I'm over here, I'll show her, I'm not going to be on the same squad as she is, I'm going out for pom-poms." To convince herself that she had made the right decision, she stated several times to Shari, "Let's do it, let's do it."

Jenna watched anxiously as the girl in front of her demonstrated the dance routine that was taught by the senior pom-pom squad one hour before the actual tryouts were to begin. Jenna began to feel nervous and thought, "I can't do this, I know I'm going to forget these steps. They didn't give me enough time to learn this routine."

As Jenna was about to walk away, the leader called, "Hey, Jenna, you're next." "I can't walk away now," Jenna fretted. They'll make fun of me and call me a loser." Jenna walked to the front of the gymnasium and waited for her signal to start. "What if I can't start when the music begins to play, what if I get off beat," Jenna asked herself.

When the music started, Jenna began to dance the routine she was taught. She was really doing well and was almost finished when she began to hear some laughter from the crowd and saw that her best friend and the same group of disgusting girls were cheering her on.

"Go Jenna. Go Jenna. Go Jenna," they screamed in unison. Jenna was surprised and taken off guard by their cheering. Jenna was so startled that she stumbled on the last turn and almost fell. She heard a few gasps and snickers from the audience. Jenna's eyes began to swell with tears. However, she quickly regained her balance and completed the routine.

Shari ran over to her and patted her on the back. "Don't worry, you were good," Shari stated. Jenna was embarrassed and humiliated as she ran from the gym. "Everybody saw me mess up, I'm such an idiot, a klutz. I should have never tried out for the squad, I'm not good enough," Jenna thought. Jenna was also convinced that her best friend and the other girls were talking and laughing behind her back. Jenna cried as she raced from the school and vowed never to dance again.

When she arrived at her house, she ran up the stairs without talking to anyone. Jenna locked her door and threw herself across the bed, weeping uncontrollably. She began to think, "I know I'm not going to make the squad. Nothing good ever happens to me. My best friend turned her back on me. Everyone in the gym laughed at me. Nothing ever works out for me. My dad never calls me. My mom is too busy to care. Maybe everyone would be better off without me. Maybe I'd be better off dead."

These thoughts continued to play over and over in her head like a broken record, and were only interrupted by the telephone ringing. Jenna paused for several seconds before answering. "Hello," she answered weakly. "Jenna? Is that you?" responded Tanya. Jenna was surprised to hear Tanya's voice. Just an hour ago she was laughing behind her back. "Yeah, it's me, what do you want?" Jenna asked suspiciously. "I was worried about you when you ran from the gym. You did such a good job with your routine, and I didn't get a chance to tell you," Tanya said.

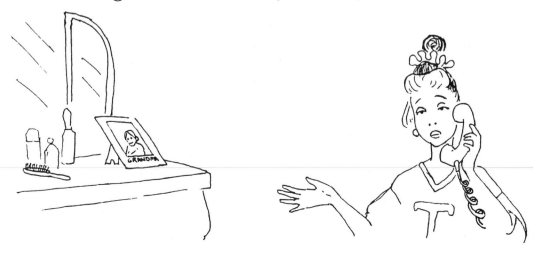

Jenna angrily stated, "Tanya, stop lying to me.
You and everybody else saw me lose my balance
and almost fall. I saw you guys laughing at me.
Everyone thinks I am a loser." Tanya went on to
explain that everyone thought she had done
well, but Jenna refused to hear it. Jenna began
to cry once again and told Tanya that she was
feeling miserable and alone. Although Tanya did
her best to comfort her, Jenna continued to cry
and state how unhappy she was with her life.
"Things at home are different since my parents
divorced, and no one seems interested in me or
in my life. I feel useless, no one cares about me.
Maybe I should run away or hurt myself."

    Tanya was very concerned by her best
friend's statements and said, "Jenna, maybe you

should talk to your mom, maybe she can help."
"My mom is too busy with work, and when I try
to talk with her, she tells me that I'll get over it.
I can't talk to her, she just doesn't understand."

Tanya had an idea. "What about Ms.
Smith, our school counselor? She talks with
kids all the time. I talked to her last year after
my grandmother died and she really helped me
talk and express my feelings. She can help you
too." "I don't think anyone can help me," Jenna
stated sadly. "Please give it a try, I'll go with you
if you want me to," Tanya replied. "Okay, I'll go

tomorrow, but will you really go with me?" Jenna
asked. "Of course, you're my best friend. See you
tomorrow," Tanya said before she hung up the
telephone. Jenna sighed with relief and started
to feel better already. "I hope Ms. Smith can
help me," she thought as she drifted off to sleep.

CHAPTER SIX

Session III: ABC Theory

Objective: To teach the child about monitoring thoughts

Introduction

Briefly review last session. Collect and discuss the creative experiment.

Agenda

- Review "Why Me? The Story of Evan" or "What's Wrong, Jenna?"

- Introduce the ABC Theory and apply concepts of it to the story.

- Discuss cognitive distortions, monitoring thoughts, and any specific issues or concerns identified by the child.

Presentation/Exercise

Referring to "Why Me? The Story of Evan" or "What's Wrong, Jenna?" ask the child to summarize his or her understanding of the story and to relate it to depression. Choose one scenario from these descriptions that will be used during the session to clarify the principles of cognitive therapy. For example:

> Evan remembers a day when he tried to kick a ball: He fell flat on his back, and everyone laughed at him. Evan was very embarrassed and felt sad. He thought, "I'm a jerk. Everyone thinks I'm stupid and clumsy."

Evan was experiencing bad self-talk, which is of course, a cognitive distortion. Evan believed that everyone laughed at him, teased him, and considered him stupid and clumsy.

Because he had these thoughts, he began to feel embarrassed and sad. No one actually called him stupid and clumsy, but Evan thought this as a result of his falling down.

You may also refer to the following example from the "What's Wrong, Jenna?" story to explain cognitive therapy concepts to older children:

> "When she arrived at her house, she ran up the stairs without talking to anyone. Jenna locked her door and threw herself across the bed, weeping uncontrollably. She began to think, 'I know I'm not going to make the squad. Nothing good ever happens to me. My best friend turned her back on me. Everyone in the gym laughed at me. Nothing ever works out for me. My dad never calls me. My mom is too busy to care. Maybe everyone would be better off without me. Maybe I'd be better off dead.'"

In the above example, Jenna also was experiencing negative self-talk as a result of seeing her situation in a distorted manner. Jenna made several negative statements as she ran from the gym. She was convinced that she would not make the squad and also believed that her best friend had turned her back on her. Due to repetitive negative self-talk, Jenna became so despondent that she began to contemplate suicide. When referring to this example, emphasize that although Jenna had stumbled and quickly regained her balance, she immediately perceived her future as a pom-pom girl as impossible. It is also important to stress that no one in the crowd at the gym told Jenna that she would not make the squad and it is highly unlikely that everyone was laughing at her.

Next, introduce the principles of cognitive therapy (the ABC Theory) as a way to help the child understand depression and its relationship to stressors, problematic situations, or other distressful life experiences for the child.

Explaining ABC

A = Activating Event. This is a situation or problem that may lead to or bring about the occurrence of negative feelings or negative perceptions. In Evan's situation, playing ball, falling down, and being teased is the event. For Jenna, the situation that provokes or influences the onset of negative self-talk are the gasps and snickers she overhears when she loses her balance during tryouts. The activating event precedes the behavior. For example, certain situations can increase or decrease the way a person feels. A child will probably feel happy and laugh when going to a circus or amusement park, and will probably feel sad and cry when visiting a sick grandparent in the hospital. Provide other examples of antecedents until the child understands.

B = Behaviors or Beliefs. These may be defined as automatic negative thoughts brought on by faulty assumptions related to the activating event. More specifically, these are beliefs or thoughts that come after events or situations. For example, the child attributes an unpleasant event to his or her own physical or moral deficits, and may see himself or herself as worthless, undesirable, ugly, inadequate, or dumb.

C = Consequences (Emotional or Behavioral). These may be referred to as events or experiences that occur based on a belief about an event. What happens next? What does the child do? How does the child feel? As an example, the child may feel more depressed, become less active, avoid activities with family or friends, or refuse to go to school.

Self-Monitoring

Self-monitoring is an important technique to teach a child who exhibits depressive symptoms. This technique involves instructing the child to monitor his or her feelings, behaviors, and most importantly, thoughts, that occur during specific situations. The older child or adolescent is often encouraged to write down his or her thoughts and feelings during the initial stages of treatment. Self-monitoring not only serves as an assessment tool for you, but it also has many other purposes, such as determining how active the child is during the week and helping the child begin to make the connections between thoughts and feelings. Most importantly, this procedure helps you understand what is happening in the child's life (Stark, et al. 1991).

In order to further clarify this technique, you may refer to "Why Me? The Story of Evan" or "What's Wrong, Jenna?" By highlighting Evan's examples of negative thoughts and bad self-talk (such as "I can't play sports," "Everyone thinks I'm stupid and clumsy," "They'll never ask me to play again"), you can help the child begin to identify his or her own negative thoughts. This will lead the child to understand and engage in the process of monitoring and changing his or her cognitive distortions. After you provide this information, instruct the child to complete the "Check Out Your Thoughts" exercise during the session.

For Group Therapy

Instruct group members to summarize the key events of "Why Me? The Story of Evan" or "What's Wrong, Jenna?" Discuss concepts of the ABC Theory with the group by presenting an example depicted in one of the stories. After going over this information with the participants, construct an ABC chart that illustrates the key components of the theory.

Another group exercise you can do is:

Describe the following hypothetical situation to the group (first, have the children close their eyes): Imagine a child around your age walking down the street alone. Several feet away, a group of kids are walking in the child's direction. One of the kids in the group turns to the others and makes a comment and they begin to laugh. Two of the kids in the group look in the first child's direction.

Instruct the group participants to open their eyes and to discuss their reactions to the hypothetical situation. Utilizing the group's responses, construct the ABC diagram. During this exercise, the following should be emphasized: A = Activating event, B = Beliefs (bad self-talk), and C = emotional/behavioral Consequences.

Feedback

Try to elicit information from the child regarding his or her overall perception about today's session.

Creative Experiment

Explain the "ABC Exercise" and the "Daily Activity Schedule."

You may experience some difficulty explaining the ABC Theory to a younger child, although it can be done with the use of concrete examples. In order to clarify this concept, the following dialogue may prove useful:

Therapist: The last time you were here we talked about Evan, the little boy who became upset at school.

Johnny: Yeah, he fell down while trying to kick a ball.

Therapist: Do you remember how he felt?

Johnny: He felt angry.

Therapist: Do you remember any other feelings?

Johnny: He also felt sad.

Therapist: You're right. Evan experienced angry and sad feelings. We are going to talk more today about what caused him to feel angry and sad. I'm going to explain how Evan's story can be explained on this ABC chart. Learning about the ABC chart is very important and should be easy to remember.

Johnny: I already know my ABCs.

Therapist: I'm sure you do, but these ABCs are different. *A* means activating event. This is a big word and you don't have to remember it. You only need to know that *A* is the problem that a child has that may cause him or her to feel sad, angry, afraid, or mad. When we talked about Evan last week, he had a problem at school that you mentioned. What was the problem?

Johnny: He fell down at school when he tried to kick the ball.

Therapist: Then what happened?

Johnny: The kids laughed at him. They were pointing at him and teasing him on the playground.

Therapist: You're right. So the activating event that we will call *A* is the problem that Evan had, which was falling down after he tried to kick the ball. *A* is what Evan thinks caused him to feel angry and sad. Now let's talk about what *B* means, since you probably understand now what *A* stands for. *B* stands for the beliefs or thoughts that a child has after the problem occurs. In other words, *B* comes after *A*. Do you remember what Evan was thinking after he fell down on the playground?

Johnny: That he was stupid.

Therapist: Yes. In the story, Evan thought, "I'm a stupid jerk; everyone thinks I'm stupid and clumsy." He also believed that no one would ever ask him to play again.

Johnny: Because the kids laughed and teased him.

Therapist: Exactly. You'll need to remember that the letter *B* stands for the beliefs and thoughts a child has about what happened to him or her. Usually these thoughts are negative, or bad, self-talk. Evan thought, "I'm stupid and clumsy" when he fell down after trying to kick the ball. Now we go to the last important letter, which is . . . ?

Johnny: C.

Therapist: Right. C stands for consequences. Consequences is also a big word that you
              won't need to remember, but the letter C is important. C means what happens
              next? What does the child do? How does the child feel after he or she has a
              problem that is upsetting him? So let's talk about Evan again. Remember, A is
              the situation or problem, so for Evan one of the problems he had was falling
              down after he tried to kick the ball. B stands for his beliefs or thoughts, what
              he was thinking. When Evan fell down, he thought, "I'm stupid and clumsy."
              In the story, what did Evan do after he had these thoughts?

Johnny: He fought with his sister and brother.

Therapist: Yes. He stated that he always argues with his brother and sister. What else did
              he do when feeling angry?

Johnny: He got real mad and went to his room.

Therapist: You're right again. C is what Evan did. He argued and went to his room. C
              also stands for the feelings he had after he fell down. Let's talk about some of
              his feelings. You mentioned them earlier.

Johnny: He felt sad.

Therapist: He also felt embarrassed.

Johnny: He felt really angry.

Therapist: Evan feels angry when he is at home. Do you know what the problem is at
              home when he feels angry?

Johnny: He gets teased and picked on.

Therapist: Evan thinks that things aren't any better at home. He not only gets teased by
              the kids at school, but also by his brother and sister. So let's take a look again
              at ABC. A is the problem. Give me some examples of B—the thoughts or beliefs
              Evan had about being teased.

Johnny: They don't like him.

Therapist: He could think that. In the story, Evan also thought that he was always picked
              on and treated unfairly. Let's read together a part of the story where Evan was
              being picked on by his sister and brother: "Evan thinks they treat him unfairly.
              Sometimes Evan tells them to shut up or yells at them." Now let's talk about
              C again. C is what Evan does or what happens next. Let's go back to the story.
              Evan does something. He tells his brother and sister to shut up. He feels angry,
              he goes to his room and shuts the door. These are examples of C, the conse-
              quences. Johnny, I'm going to give you a quick review. We will start with A.
              A is the situation or problem. Do you remember what A was for Evan?

Johnny: Yeah, he fell down and got teased.

Therapist: Good. Now let's review B. B stands for the thoughts and beliefs. Give me a
              couple of the thoughts that Evan had. What was Evan thinking?

Johnny: "I am dumb and stupid. No one wants to be my friend."

Therapist: Good job. Okay, last but not least is C, the consequences. Do you remember
              what C means?

Johnny: Umh . . .

Therapist: That's okay, C is a little more difficult to remember. C is what happens next. What did Evan do?

Johnny: Oh yeah, now I remember. He got angry and ran to his room. He also started yelling at his sister and brother.

Therapist: You're absolutely right.

As previously indicated, the ABC Theory is difficult to explain to a younger child, therefore it is important to give concrete examples and review these examples several times during the session. To further confirm the child's understanding of the ABC process, encourage the child to identify his or her own personal problem or situation in terms of ABC. Refer to the following dialogue for clarification:

Therapist: Now I would like you to think about a problem or situation that happened to you. Your example will let me know if I did a good job of teaching you ABC. I need you to think of a time when you were feeling sad, angry, or down about something that happened to you at school or at home.

Johnny: I don't remember.

Therapist: Take your time and think a little bit about a time when you were feeling pretty ticked off or upset about something that happened to you. It might be helpful to think of a situation that happened recently, you know, a few days ago or so.

Johnny: Well, I got mad at this boy in school who pushed me in the lunch line. He said I cut in front of him and I didn't. I pushed him back and the lunch lady hollered at me.

Therapist: So what happened next?

Johnny: I told her that he pushed me first and she just yelled for me to move on.

Therapist: How did you feel about the situation?

Johnny: I felt mad.

Therapist: Who were you mad at?

Johnny: I was mad at the boy who pushed me and that mean, old lunch lady.

Therapist: Johnny, let's take a look at your situation and use the "ABC Exercise" chart that we talked about. Instead of talking about Evan, we can use your situation. Seems like you experienced feeling mad just like Evan did when he fell in the playground.

Johnny: I was real mad. I wanted to punch that boy, but I didn't want to get in trouble or get suspended.

Therapist: You made the right decision. Now let's decide what goes in the A column. Remember, A is the problem that happens to you. What was A for you, Johnny?

Johnny: That boy pushed me in the cafeteria line and said I cut in front of him. He made me get hollered at. I pushed him for pushing me first.

Therapist: Johnny, I'll be writing down what you say in these columns so you can take this chart home to review. This will help you remember what goes under A, B, and C. Okay, what goes under the B column? Remember, B stands for the beliefs or thoughts that a child has. Evan thought that he was stupid and clumsy when he fell down.

Johnny: I thought that boy didn't like me and wanted to get me in trouble. The lunch lady didn't like me either because she hollered at me and didn't holler at the boy who started it. I'm always getting hollered at when it's not my fault.

Therapist: This situation, *A*, caused you to have a lot of *B* thoughts. You started thinking, "No one likes me," and you also thought, "I am always getting hollered at." Am I right?

Johnny: Yes.

Therapist: Now let's go to column *C* on the chart. As we talked about earlier, *C* means consequences. What happens next? What does the child do? How does the child feel? Johnny, what happened after you and the boy got into a pushing match?

Johnny: I got hollered at.

Therapist: How did you feel?

Johnny: Angry.

Therapist: Did you have any other feelings?

Johnny: I felt a little scared.

Therapist: Tell me about what was causing you to feel scared.

Johnny: I thought I was going to have to fight. Then I thought I was going to get in trouble. You know, get suspended.

Therapist: So you had many thoughts and beliefs going through your head. I am going to write down these new thoughts under the *B* column. Now let's take a look at the *C* column again. You felt angry and scared because of the thoughts you had. You had these thoughts because you got pushed and also because you got hollered at by the lunch lady. After you went through the lunch line, did you do anything else?

Johnny: I sat down at the table with the other kids.

Therapist: Did you behave any differently when you were with your friends? Did you still feel angry or scared?

Johnny: I didn't eat all my lunch. I didn't feel like talking very much. I was still mad but not scared.

Therapist: You just gave me more examples of *C*, the consequences. What you did was you didn't eat all your lunch and you weren't talking as much with your friends. You were also still feeling mad about the situation. I am going to put what you said under column *C*.

Explaining the ABC Theory to an adolescent will most likely be easier. The following example demonstrates how the therapist educates Cindy about these important concepts:

Therapist: The last time you were here we talked about the story "What's Wrong, Jenna?" Do you remember what happened to Jenna?

Cindy: No, I don't remember. What's that have to do with me anyway?

Therapist: Well, that's a good point, Cindy, but I think it will become clear to you once we review the basic points of the story. Jenna was the girl who was feeling upset because her girlfriends were teasing her about getting a good grade, and later that day she messed up during pom-pom tryouts. Do you remember how she felt?

Cindy: Yeah. She was bummed out.

Therapist: You're right. Jenna was feeling very sad and down on herself.

Note: If the child continues to seem uninterested in the story of Jenna, ask the child for an example of a time when he or she felt upset or "bummed out." When using the child's own example, it is important to obtain as much information as possible from the child and continue with the following dialogue for direction:

Therapist: Now let's look at Jenna's situation (or teen's own example) and explain it on this "ABC Exercise" chart. The ABC chart is a very important and helpful tool to help us become more aware of how certain situations can "activate," or lead, us to feel and behave in a certain way. Does this sound okay with you?

Cindy: Yeah, but I'm still not sure how this will help me with my problems.

Therapist: For many teens, the "ABC Exercise" chart can help them get better control and understanding of how and why they feel the way they do. Okay, let's take a look at this chart. *A* means the activating event, or in other words, the situation or problem that is causing the person to feel sad, angry, or mad. For Jenna, the situation was being teased and laughed at by her friends and messing up at the tryouts. (If you're using the teen's own example, ask him or her to restate the problem situation.) Does this make sense?

Cindy: Yeah, so what's *B* and *C*?

Therapist: Okay, good question. Let's go on to *B*. *B* stands for the beliefs and thoughts a person has. Do you remember what happened after Jenna stumbled at the tryouts? What was she thinking?

Cindy: I don't remember exactly, but I think she was thinking she was a real klutz.

Therapist: You're right. Let's look together at this piece of her story. Cindy, why don't you read this section aloud.

Cindy: Okay. "Shari ran over to her and patted her on the back. 'Don't worry, you were good,' Shari stated. Jenna was embarrassed and humiliated as she ran from the gym. 'Everybody saw me mess up, I'm such an idiot, a klutz. I should have never tried out for the squad, I'm not good enough,' Jenna thought. Jenna was also convinced that her best friend and the other girls were talking and laughing behind her back. Jenna cried as she raced from the school and vowed never to dance again."

Therapist: So, it seems like Jenna had several thoughts running through her mind. Cindy, can you identify any of the negative thoughts that she had?

Cindy: Well, I already said that she thought she was a klutz. She also thought she was an idiot and that everybody was laughing at her.

Therapist: You just identified Jenna's negative beliefs or bad self-talk. Let's go on and look at C. C stands for the consequences that follow. Consequences mean how the person feels and what the person does. In the Jenna story, how was she feeling?

Cindy: She was upset and sad. She was probably a little ticked off, too.

Therapist: Exactly. She was feeling very unhappy and probably alone. She may have also felt a little angry like you suggested—Uh, "ticked off."

The following dialogue highlights Cindy's understanding of the ABC Theory using a personal situation:

Therapist: Now, Cindy, we have just reviewed the principles of the ABC Theory and how it could be applied to Jenna's story. Let's review the ABC Theory again, but let's use one of your own examples of a recent time in which you found yourself experiencing strong feelings about a situation. Okay?

Cindy: Okay, but I can't think of anything.

Therapist: Well, let's put our heads together and think of a recent time you were feeling either real sad or angry.

Cindy: Well, I was real mad at my mom this past Saturday night.

Therapist: Okay, let's look more closely at the situation. Can you tell me how the situation began?

Cindy: I wanted to go all-night bowling on Saturday night, but my mom ruined the whole thing! On Friday, when I first asked her if I could go, she told me that I could. For no reason, an hour before I was supposed to leave the house, she changed her mind and told me I couldn't go.

Therapist: That must have been very disappointing! What happened to make your mom suddenly change her mind?

Cindy: She made a big deal out of nothing! She found out there would be no adult supervision and that put her right over the edge! We got into a huge argument.

Therapist: Cindy, I'm sorry to hear that you had such a big argument. You did a nice job explaining it to me. Let's take a look at your situation and use the "ABC Exercise" chart. Instead of talking about Jenna we can use your situation. Let's decide what would go in the A column.

Cindy: The situation—which was my mom telling me at the last minute that I couldn't go to all-night bowling.

Therapist: Exactly. Let's write this down so it will help you remember what goes under each column. (Teens should be encouraged to write information in the appropriate columns.) Let's move on. What was B—the thoughts and beliefs you had going through your mind at the time? Can you think back and remember what you were thinking at the time?

Cindy: Yeah, that's easy. I was thinking she never lets me do anything fun. She lets my brother do everything. They treat me like a little baby. She makes me so sick. I wish I could live with someone else. I'd live almost anywhere. My mom really gets on my nerves.

Therapist: Wow, you had several thoughts and beliefs. You did a nice job remembering what *B* refers to. Some of the thoughts that you had can also be referred to as bad, or negative, self-talk. Bad self-talk can occur during many situations in life. When a person engages in bad self-talk, he or she may feel sad, angry, down in the dumps, or disappointed with himself or herself or the people around him or her. The bad self-talk often adds to the unpleasant feelings you already have. In other words, when you are feeling unhappy about something and you continue to have negative thoughts and use bad self-talk, it causes you to feel even more unhappy. Often, the bad self-talk intensifies and worsens the initial unpleasant feelings that you had. One negative thought leads to another negative thought, and over and over, like a small snowball rolling along picking up more and more snow until it's a huge snowball. If the person has several negative thoughts or a lot of bad self-talk, he or she may feel overwhelmed by the growing size of the snowball. Does this make sense to you?

Cindy: Yeah. I think I definitely have times when I snowball.

Therapist: Okay, well let's get back to your example. In your situation you were clearly feeling angry. After you had the thoughts, "She never lets me do anything, she lets my brother do everything," "She treats me like a little baby," "She makes me sick, I wish I could live with someone else," how did you feel then? Do you remember if your self-talk helped you feel better or worse?

Cindy: I sure didn't feel happy. I felt worse. I was furious and really pissed off. I felt like my blood was boiling.

Therapist: You and I will be spending more time talking about self-talk, both bad self-talk and good self-talk. We'll talk more about "snowballs" and how to prevent them from getting too big. For now, let's get back to finishing our discussion of how your situation can be explained with the ABC Theory. Let's summarize what we've identified so far for the chart. Using your example, Cindy, what was *A*, or the activating event?

Cindy: Being told at the last minute that I couldn't go to all-night bowling.

Therapist: And what was *B*—the beliefs and thoughts you had following this situation?

Cindy: I thought she never lets me do anything, my brother gets to do everything, she treats me like a baby. Umh, she makes me sick. I wish I could live with someone else, anybody, anywhere.

Therapist: And what was *C*—the consequences or what you did or felt?

Cindy: I got so angry that I screamed at my mom and ran to my room. I didn't come out until the next morning. My dad grounded me for the rest of the weekend because I screamed at my mom.

These dialogues may appear to be somewhat lengthy and repetitive (particularly the dialogue between the therapist and Johnny, who is a much younger child); however, it is imperative to review the key concepts so that the child gains some understanding. Your task is to help the child begin to see the connection between *A* (situation), *B* (beliefs, thoughts), and *C* (consequences). It also may be useful to begin to use the concept of bad self-talk when referring to the *B* statements. As was indicated previously in this manual, feelings of sadness, anger, frustration, and so on, are brought on by negative self-talk that the child engages in as a result of the problem situation or event.

Check Out Your Thoughts

Name _____   Date_____

> DIRECTIONS: Read each statement carefully and decide how you
> would think about yourself if this situation occurred. Circle the
> number that best describes your thoughts. There are no right or
> wrong answers.

1	2	3	4
just like me	a lot like me	a little like me	nothing like me

---

1. You were not invited to a birthday party given
    by one of your classmates. Would you think, "I
    wasn't invited because no one likes me"?   1 2 3 4

2. You studied for a test and got a D on it. Would
    you think, "I'm just a dummy, I study and never get
    good grades"?   1 2 3 4

3. Someone tells you that they like your new outfit.
    Would you think, "I don't believe it; besides, what's
    so great about this outfit anyway"?   1 2 3 4

4. You were playing a game of Monopoly with a group of
    friends and you lost. Everyone laughs and
    teases you about being in last place. Would you
    think, "I've never been good at playing board games"?   1 2 3 4

5. You and about fifty other kids try out for the school
    play. You rehearsed your lines for several days;
    however, you only get a small role. Would you
    think, "They didn't think I was good enough and just
    felt sorry for me, so they gave me this dumb, small part." 1 2 3 4

6. You are trying out for cheerleading and someone yells,
    "You're too clumsy and off beat to be a cheerleader."
    Would you think, "I'll never make the squad because
    I have two left feet"?   1 2 3 4

7. Your best friends do not choose you to be on their
    kickball team. Would you think, "They do not like me
    anymore because I'm not a good player"?   1 2 3 4

8. You called everyone you could think of to go with you
    to the movies, but everyone had other plans. Would
    you think, "No one cares enough about me, I don't have
    real friends"?   1 2 3 4

Name_____

ABC Exercise

Date_____

A = SITUATION	B = BELIEFS / THOUGHTS	C = CONSEQUENCE

ABC Exercise

Name_____   Date_____

| A = SITUATION | B = BELIEFS / THOUGHTS | C = CONSEQUENCE |

Daily Activity Schedule

Name _____   Date _____

DIRECTIONS: Indicate in each column below at least three activities during each time of day. Also indicate the emotion (happy, sad, angry, etc.) felt during each activity.
Rate intensity of emotions from 1-10

Morning		Afternoon		Evening		Bedtime	
1.		1.		1.		1.	
Emotion_____	Number_____	Emotion_____	Number_____	Emotion_____	Number_____	Emotion_____	Number_____
2.		2.		2.		2.	
Emotion_____	Number_____	Emotion_____	Number_____	Emotion_____	Number_____	Emotion_____	Number_____
3.		3.		3.		3.	
Emotion_____	Number_____	Emotion_____	Number_____	Emotion_____	Number_____	Emotion_____	Number_____

CHAPTER SEVEN

Session IV:
Bad Self-Talk vs. Good Self-Talk

Objective: To help the child eliminate cognitive distortions

Introduction

Briefly review the last session and obtain feedback from the child about his or her understanding of ABC Theory. Reintroduce the ABC Theory and present techniques using this
concept.

Agenda

- Review the ABC Theory.
- Role-play problem situations.
- Identify the child's specific issues or concerns.

Presentation/Exercise

Ask the child to reflect on recent or past problems that occurred in the home or school
environment. If the child doesn't come up with a problem situation, present a hypothetical
problem situation that closely reflects his or her experience (refer to child's psychiatric his-
tory, psychosocial evaluation, target behaviors, or treatment plan). You may also use the
child's creative experiments. Have the child define the problem situations in terms of ABC
Theory to assess his or her understanding of and further clarify this concept.

Rational Responses

Rational responses are positive thoughts or good self-talk. These are words the child can say to himself or herself that will eliminate or decrease negative thoughts, beliefs, and feelings. Positive self-talk or good self-talk gives the child the opportunity to feel good about himself or herself. You should emphasize that it is okay to say good things about oneself, and it is also good to recognize what one does well (Barth 1985). Utilize "Why Me? The Story of Evan" or "What's Wrong, Jenna?" to elicit positive thoughts and good self-talk.

By this session the child is probably quite familiar with the story of Evan or Jenna. In clinical settings in which these stories or similar ones were utilized, it was apparent that a child who exhibited depressive symptoms, including low self-esteem, was able to identify with the character in the story. It is also important to note that the child was quite familiar with the negative language, or bad self-talk, that the character used in the stories and admitted using similar language when problem situations occurred in his or her daily life. On the other hand, the child had difficulty coming up with positive statements, or good self-talk, when encouraged to do so during the therapy session. It is therefore quite important to educate the child about the concept of good self-talk and provide examples of positive statements. To clarify how this concept can be explained to a child please refer to the following examples:

Therapist: During the last couple of sessions we talked about bad self-talk and how this type of talking and thinking brings about feelings of anger and sadness. Bad self-talk tends to make you feel miserable and bad inside, and sometimes do things that you may not feel good about. Johnny, can you give me some examples of bad self-talk that a child your age may use when a problem comes up at home, at school, or even in your neighborhood? If you can, think about a time during the past few days where you might have used bad self-talk.

Johnny: I was mad at my brother because he stepped on my model car I was trying to fix.

Therapist: So you were feeling mad about what happened?

Johnny: Yeah.

Therapist: Now you remember your feelings are often caused by the thoughts you are having. When your little brother stepped on your model car, you probably started having these negative thoughts. What type of thoughts were going through your head when your brother stepped on the car?

Johnny: He did it on purpose.

Therapist: What other type of negative things did you say to yourself?

Johnny: He's always messing up my stuff. He never gets in trouble.

Therapist: Any other thoughts?

Johnny: He doesn't like me.

Therapist: Everything that you just reported are examples of bad self-talk and this talk made you feel angry. If you begin to use good self-talk when a problem happens to you, your feelings may be different. You may not feel as angry or sad. You may not want to hit your little brother or do other things that might get you into trouble with your parents.

Johnny: I did hit my brother when he stepped on my car. I didn't hurt him though. I was just mad. My mom yelled at me, but I didn't get into trouble.

Therapist: It's okay to feel angry when something upsets you, but it's not okay to hit. When you begin to learn more about good self-talk and begin to practice positive things you can say to yourself to get rid of and change bad self-talk, you won't need to hit your little brother when he does things that get on your nerves. Okay?

Johnny: Okay, I guess.

Therapist: Now let's talk about good self-talk. Good self-talk is a rational response. You won't need to remember the term "rational responses"—that's just a grown-up way to say positive thoughts, or good self-talk. Good self-talk includes positive words that a child can say to himself or herself. These positive thoughts, good self-talk, can help a child eliminate, decrease or get rid of negative thoughts, negative beliefs, and negative talk, which is called . . . ?

Johnny: Bad self-talk?

Therapist: You're right. Negative self-talk is another name for bad self-talk. However, when you try to get rid of bad self-talk by saying positive things to yourself, what kind of talk are you using?

Johnny: Good self-talk.

Therapist: You're doing great. You already know the difference between good and bad self-talk. Now let's talk about our friend Evan. He used a lot of bad self-talk and had many negative thoughts about himself. What was some of the bad self-talk that Evan had?

Johnny: No one liked him. He had no friends. He couldn't kick the ball.

Therapist: Any other bad self-talk?

Johnny: He had a real bad thought.

Therapist: What thought was that?

Johnny: He wanted to hurt himself.

Therapist: You're right, Johnny. Evan talked to himself in a negative way, which is bad self-talk. If we could change or replace some of Evan's bad self-talk with good self-talk, what might Evan say?

Johnny: I don't know.

Therapist: I'll help you out a bit. You just said that one of Evan's negative thoughts was that no one liked him. Because he believed that no one liked him, he felt angry and sad. Do you believe that no one at all liked Evan?

Johnny: That's what he said in the story. Not even his brother or sister liked him.

Therapist: What do you really think about what he thought? Do you really believe that his brother and sister don't like him?

Johnny: They probably like him sometimes.

Therapist: So if his brother and sister like him sometimes should he use bad self-talk and say that no one likes him?

Johnny: No. His mom and dad probably like him.

Therapist: You're doing great here. You've already come up with some good self-talk for Evan. You stated that his mom and dad probably like him. So when Evan is feeling sad and angry and believes that everyone dislikes him, he could say to himself, "That's not true, my parents like me." He can also say, "Sometimes my brother and sister like me." This is more good self-talk. Now let's get back to the problem you recently had with your brother. You stated that he stepped on your model car.

Johnny: Yeah. I was just about done putting it together and he stepped on it.

Therapist: Tell me more about what happened. Did your brother just walk over to you and step on your car for no reason?

Johnny: He was running through the living room and stepped on it.

Therapist: So it may have been an accident.

Johnny: No, it wasn't an accident, he did it on purpose. He always breaks my toys. I told you before.

Therapist: I know you did. You also reported feeling angry with your brother and having bad self-talk. When you say things like "My brother always breaks my toys," or "He never gets into trouble, and he does things on purpose," these thoughts make you feel even angrier. You are already upset that your model car was stepped on, but you feel even more angry by using bad self-talk. What I want you to think about now is how you could change some of your bad self-talk to good self-talk when your brother does things that upset or anger you. Can you give me an example of good self-talk?

Johnny: Umh . . . He didn't mean to step on my car?

Therapist: Okay, so it was probably an accident. Why do you think he didn't mean to do it?

Johnny: He was running very fast and didn't see it. He's only four years old.

Therapist: Johnny, it probably was an accident, huh?

Johnny: I guess so. He probably didn't do it on purpose. He just wasn't looking where he was going.

Therapist: Johnny, you're starting to use good self-talk. Instead of saying, "My brother stepped on my car on purpose," or "He always steps on and messes up my things," you stated that he was running very fast and didn't see it. When you think about what happened in this way, you might not feel as angry. I also want you to think about some other bad self-talk that you used when you were talking about your brother earlier. You mentioned that he always messes up and breaks your toys. Do you mean that you and your brother have never played nicely together? He breaks all your toys when he is around you?

Johnny: No, he doesn't always break my things.

Therapist: So there are times when you don't mind sharing your toys with your brother?

Johnny: Yes.

Therapist: You also stated that your brother never gets in trouble. He must be perfect. I know a lot of kids, even younger ones, that sometimes get in trouble with their parents when they misbehave.

Johnny: He's not perfect. He's bad sometimes. My grandmother put him in time-out yesterday for using a bad word.

At this point, you may continue to point out examples from the child's own experience or problem situation in which negative self-talk was indicated. Your primary task is to help the child identify when he or she is using negative talk to rationalize his or her perceptions of the activating event. Younger children in particular may benefit from very specific, concrete examples, whereas adolescents may be more able to identify the use of bad self-talk on their own. When a child is reluctant or having difficulty identifying problem situations during the course of treatment, use situations that the child may have disclosed during previous sessions. To further promote the child's self-awareness and understanding of the rational response/good self-talk concept, you may want to do some role-playing. Here are some examples that may be presented:

o I got a D on my report card and might fail.

o I am ugly because I have acne.

o I feel sad every day because no one likes me.

o I have no friends and feel lonely.

o I should jump out the window and die because I feel hurt and angry.

The following dialogue shows how to use these role-playing examples:

Therapist: Oftentimes children like yourself begin to feel sad and disappointed with themselves when a situation occurs that brings about the use of bad self-talk. I have a couple of problems written on cards that can cause a child to become upset, angry, sad, or depressed. As we talked about in earlier sessions, bad self-talk is something that we tell ourselves that may make us feel angry, sad, or disappointed when something happens in our lives. When this happens we need to think differently. We need to work harder at changing these thoughts. In order to change these thoughts, we need to replace them with more positive thoughts, or good self-talk. What I want you to do now is to help the child described on the card come up with good self-talk so that he or she can feel better about himself or herself, okay?

Johnny: (picks card from the pile and gives it to the therapist) How about this one?

Therapist: Why don't you read what the problem is. Then we can role-play, which means act out the problem situation.

Johnny: Okay. "I feel sad every day because no one likes me."

Therapist: What do you think might be causing this child to feel sad every day?

Johnny: I don't know.

Therapist: Since we are going to role-play this situation, we need to think about the situation that is making the child feel sad. You don't have to use your own situation; you can make up one. If you need some help, I also may have some ideas for us to talk about.

Johnny: Maybe his best friend moved away and he has no one to play with.

Therapist:	That's a very good problem situation. When a good friend moves away, it is very common for a child to experience many feelings. What do you think the child in this situation may be feeling?
Johnny:	He probably feels sad or maybe angry because he has no one in the neighborhood to play with.
Therapist:	Johnny, you did a good job identifying feelings that the child probably feels as a result of his friend moving away. Since the child is having these feelings of sadness and anger, he is probably using what kind of self-talk?
Johnny:	Bad self-talk.
Therapist:	Right. What kind of talk should he use to feel better and not feel so sad and angry?
Johnny:	Good self-talk.
Therapist:	You're on a roll. Okay, now let's make this situation more fun and interesting by role-playing the situation. Let's pretend that the boy whose friend moved away is sitting on his porch at home. He's all alone until another child who lives down the street asks him why he is sitting by himself. Now this is the fun part. You decide if you want to be the child who is feeling sad or angry or the child who lives down the street.
Johnny:	Who are you going to be?
Therapist:	I'll be whoever you want me to be.
Johnny:	(*laughs*) You be the boy on the steps.
Therapist:	Okay. So let's start off by pretending that I'm sitting on the steps and you come up to me and say hello or something.
Johnny:	I don't know what to say. You start.
Therapist:	Just pretend to walk over to me and say hello and I'll help you out. Remember there is no right or wrong way to do this. We're pretending to help this boy feel better.
Johnny:	Okay ... Hi. Why are you sitting by yourself?
Therapist:	Because I have no friends and no one likes me.
Johnny:	I'll be your friend.
Therapist:	I don't believe you. No one wants to be my friend.
Johnny:	I'll play with you if you want.
Therapist:	No one plays with me. If they do, they end up moving away like my best friend did.
Johnny:	You can make new friends.
Therapist:	No one really wants to be my friend. They'll play with me for a little while and then leave me to play with other kids.
Johnny:	I won't do that. You can come over to my house to play.
Therapist:	Do you really want to be my friend?

Johnny: Yes, and you can help me build my model car.

Therapist: I'm not good at building model cars. I break everything I touch. I can't do anything right.

Johnny: *(giggles)* Yes, you can. I'll show you how to put an easy model together.

Therapist: Okay, but you'll probably make fun of me when I make a mistake. All the kids make fun of me.

Johnny: I won't make fun of you. I want to be your friend.

Therapist: Let's stop here. Johnny, you were great. You were trying very hard to make me feel accepted. Now let's talk about the role-playing for a little bit. When I was acting as the kid who felt lonely, what type of talk was I using?

Johnny: Bad self-talk.

Therapist: Exactly. I was saying things like "No one wants to play with me." "No one wants to be my friend. All the kids make fun of me."

Johnny: You said that you couldn't put models together.

Therapist: Yeah, I used a lot of bad self-talk. Now I want you to help me change my bad self-talk to good self-talk. When I was pretending to be the lonely child, I said something like if you play with me you will probably move away like my best friend did. Johnny, what could I say that would make me feel better?

Johnny: "Maybe he won't move away like my other friend did. I can make a new best friend."

Therapist: Okay, so as the child, I can say something like, "Just because my best friend moved away doesn't mean that I can't make new friends." Let's take a look at another example of bad self-talk that can be changed to good self-talk. Remember when you asked me to come over to your house to help you build a model car?

Johnny: Yeah.

Therapist: What did I say?

Johnny: You said you can't build model cars because you break things.

Therapist: Yeah. I said that I break everything that I touch. What do you think about what I said?

Johnny: You were talking bad.

Therapist: What could I have said that would be more positive, or good self-talk?

Johnny: I don't know ... Umh ...

Therapist: Remember I said that I can't build model cars.

Johnny: You could probably build an easy one.

Therapist: Okay, so instead of saying I can't build model cars, I could say I can probably build an easy one or I'll try if you'll help me. What about when I said that I break everything I touch?

Johnny: Nobody breaks everything. You're not a baby.

Therapist:	(*laughs*) You're right, no one breaks everything that they touch, not even babies. So instead of saying "I break everything that I touch," which is bad self-talk, I can say, "I don't break everything that I touch." So what type of talk am I now using?
Johnny:	Good self-talk.
Therapist:	Now let's do a quick review and talk a little bit about the connection between bad and good self-talk and feelings. Although we were pretending, what feelings do you think I had when I was using bad self-talk?
Johnny:	You were feeling sad because you had no friends and no one would play with you.
Therapist:	You're right. I kept thinking that no one would play with me and that everyone would move away. Because I used bad self-talk, I felt sad. But when you pretended to be the boy down the street who wanted to play with me, you helped me change the way I was thinking and feeling. You helped me begin to use good self-talk. You invited me to your house. You told me that I could probably build an easy model and a lot of other nice things that made me begin to think and feel differently. I began to use good self-talk. When I started to think more positively and use good self-talk, what feelings do you think I might have had?
Johnny:	Not sad.
Therapist:	So if I am no longer feeling sad and lonely, what other feelings may I have?
Johnny:	Happy, because you have a new friend?
Therapist:	I probably will be feeling a lot better and happy that someone in my neighborhood wants to play with me and be my new friend. I know I won't be feeling as sad as I was before you invited me to play with you.

During this session, the therapist used a hypothetical problem situation taken from a card to further explore the child's understanding of the bad and good self-talk concepts. Through role-playing, you can assist a child in seeing that an upsetting or problematic situation can be modified, thereby reducing bad self-talk and unpleasant feelings. To further enhance the child's understanding of the importance of utilizing good self-talk when problem situations arise in his or her own life, try to elicit from the child a personal situation that occurred recently. Refer to the following example, in which the therapist refers to a conversation that occurred with Johnny during a previous session:

Therapist:	How about some more role-playing, but this time let's use a problem situation of yours.
Johnny:	Okay.
Therapist:	Do you remember when you told me about the time you got into a shoving match with the boy in the school cafeteria?
Johnny:	Yeah, he pushed me and I pushed him back.
Therapist:	I recall that he was trying to push in front of you and that upset you. Am I remembering the situation in the way it happened?
Johnny:	Kind of. He said I tried to push in front of him, but I didn't. I got hollered at by the lunch lady when I pushed him back.

Therapist:	Now I remember. You did tell me that the boy accused you of trying to get in front of him and he pushed you out of the way. Am I correct?
Johnny:	Yeah. I pushed him back because he pushed me first.
Therapist:	How about role-playing this situation? This time I want you to be yourself. Let's pretend that you are standing in line. (*Therapist will set the scene by encouraging the child to take a place in line, and so on.*) Now I will be the boy who said that you cut in front of him. I want you to think about what thoughts you were having when this happened. Okay?
Johnny:	Okay.
Therapist:	Let's start the role-playing now. (*Therapist pretends to push in front of the child.*) Hey! You're trying to get in front of me. Get out of my way. (*Therapist pretends to shove Johnny.*)
Johnny:	What are you trying to do? I was here first. Get out of my way.
Therapist:	You get out of my way. You just cut in front of me. (*Therapist pretends to shove child again.*)
Johnny:	No, I didn't. I was here first. (*Johnny shoves back.*)
Therapist:	Johnny, let's stop this action for a minute. You're doing a good job. Now I want to change my character. Instead of being the boy who pushed in front of you, I am going to be the lunch lady who yells at you. Okay? I'll start now: Johnny (*loud voice*), what do you think you're doing? No pushing allowed in the cafeteria.
Johnny:	He pushed me first. Why don't you holler at him?
Therapist:	I saw you push him. Keep the line moving.
Johnny:	But he started it.
Therapist:	I don't want to hear one more word out of you. Now move along. No more arguing. Now let's stop again and talk about how you might be feeling and what your thoughts are.
Johnny:	This is fun. You made me laugh. You sounded like that lunch lady.
Therapist:	Good. I'm glad I did a good job.
Johnny:	She made me so mad.
Therapist:	Okay, so she made you angry.
Johnny:	Yeah.
Therapist:	What thoughts were going through your head when she hollered at you?
Johnny:	She's not fair. She likes the other boy better than me. She always picks on me.
Therapist:	Any other thoughts you might have had when she hollered at you?
Johnny:	She just doesn't like me.
Therapist:	What kind of self-talk are you using?

Johnny: I know. Bad self-talk.

Therapist: So now you have to get rid of it by using what type of self-talk?

Johnny: Good self-talk.

Therapist: Now let's go over some of the bad self-talk that you just reported. How about starting with the thought "She doesn't like me"? How do you know that she doesn't like you?

Johnny: Because she hollered at me and didn't holler at the other boy.

Therapist: Johnny, do you really believe that the lunch lady doesn't like you because she yelled at you? Has she ever come up to you to tell you that she doesn't like you?

Johnny: No.

Therapist: Has she ever told you that she likes the other boy better than you?

Johnny: No.

Therapist: Have you heard the lunch lady holler at other kids besides you?

Johnny: Sometimes.

Therapist: Does the lunch lady holler at you all the time?

Johnny: No, not all the time.

Therapist: Okay, so let's think this through. When people yell or holler at one another, what might be going on?

Johnny: Well, it means that they don't like each other.

Therapist: Well, it could mean that, but let's look at some other reasons why a person may yell. What could be another reason why the lunch lady yelled at you?

Johnny: I don't know.

Therapist: Let's put on our thinking caps, okay?

Johnny: Okay.

Therapist: Maybe she hollered at you because she was in a cranky and irritable mood and was tired of standing on her feet serving you kids lunch.

Johnny: Maybe her feet were tired; she is kind of old.

Therapist: Johnny, she may have hollered at you because she was cranky, irritable, tired, and old, but maybe she hollered at you because she did not see the other boy push you first. What do you think about that possibility?

Johnny: Maybe.

Therapist: Johnny, I realize that this was a tough situation for you. No one likes being hollered at. Because you used bad self-talk, you began to feel even more angry that the boy pushed you and didn't get caught or hollered at. If you had used good self-talk when this problem occurred you might not have felt as angry. Now let's practice some good self-talk that you can use if this situation happens again. Okay?

Johnny: Okay.

Therapist: During tough situations, when you get hollered at or feel picked on, what else can you say that would help you feel less angry or sad? Again let's remember, Johnny, good self-talk uses words that will help you keep your unpleasant feelings from getting out of control. I'll start for you. Your good self-talk could be, "Maybe the lunch lady was in a bad mood today and was feeling tired and cranky, because she doesn't holler at me every day." Okay. Now you think of an example of good self-talk.

Johnny: Sometimes she's okay because she gives me extra ice cream.

Therapist: So what you are saying, Johnny, is that she sometimes gives you extra goodies and has been nice to you?

Johnny: Yeah, sometimes she's nice and doesn't holler.

Therapist: Johnny, you're starting to use good self-talk. You just said that she is nice sometimes, doesn't holler, and also gives you extra ice cream. So when she is in a bad mood and hollers at you, you can say to yourself, "She doesn't always holler at me, she may be in a bad mood, she is sometimes nice to me and even gives me extra ice cream." Okay? Johnny, learning to use good self-talk is often difficult for kids. You're doing a pretty good job in learning how to get rid of your bad self-talk by coming up with some examples of good self-talk.

For Group Therapy

Give the group three hypothetical situations developed by you prior to the group session and instruct them to select one to role-play. The children who volunteer or who are chosen to participate in the enactment are encouraged to use bad self-talk. Ten to fifteen minutes should be given for the participants to practice the role-play before acting out the situation in front of the other group members. Instruct the rest of the group members to identify examples of bad self-talk expressed during the role-play. Once the role-play is completed, ask the group to substitute the bad self-talk with good self-talk.

For the adolescent, rational responses can also be explained as positive thoughts, or good self-talk. As was indicated in the above examples with the younger child, rational responses are words or phrases that the teen can say to himself or herself to help eliminate or decrease negative thoughts, beliefs, and feelings. You can teach the teen how to "coach" himself or herself through difficult situations by utilizing positive, or good, self-talk. It is therefore quite important to educate the teen about the concept of good self-talk and provide examples of positive statements. You can use the following step-by-step process:

1. Identify problem situation.

2. Elicit child's view of the problem situation.

3. Ask for the sequence of what happened.

4. Guide discussion to how the child felt (feels) and how others may have felt (feels).

5. Ask for one thing child might do to solve the problem.

6. Ask what might happen next if he or she did that.

7. Guide talk to facilitate child's evaluation of that solution.

8. Encourage thought of other solutions.

9. Encourage the child to try out his or her ideas (perhaps in a role-playing exercise).

10. Ask for possible obstacles (in older children).

11. Talk of a step-by-step plan (in older children).

From: Spivack, G., J. Platt, and M. Shure (1976).

The following is an example role-play clarifying how this concept can be explained to a teen:

Therapist: The last few times you were here, we talked about the concepts of bad self-talk and good self-talk. In Jenna's story, do you remember some of the examples of her bad self-talk?

Cindy: Yeah, she was "bagging" on herself by saying things like "I'm an idiot."

Therapist: What are some examples of good self-talk Jenna could have used that may have helped her feel better?

Cindy: I'm not sure, but maybe she could have had thoughts like, "I'm okay," "Things will work out," "Everyone makes mistakes sometimes."

Therapist: Good job! Those are great examples of good self-talk! I bet Jenna would have felt much better with thoughts like that. Do you think it would have made her feel totally, completely better?

Cindy: Probably not . . . maybe just not as bad.

Therapist: I think you're right—good self-talk doesn't necessarily make the person suddenly feel great, but good self-talk will help diminish or decrease the bad feelings as well as help the person gain some understanding or a better perspective of the situation. Now, it's important for you and me to focus on helping you learn to "catch" yourself when you are having bad self-talk and to help you replace your bad self-talk with rational responses, or good self-talk. Okay?

Cindy: Yeah, that makes sense, but how do we do that?

Therapist: Good question. Let's start by thinking of a recent time in which you were experiencing intense feelings of sadness or anger.

Cindy: What about the time a few weeks ago when I was so mad at my mother about all-night bowling?

Therapist: Oh yeah, that's a good example for us to look at. Let's role-play, or act out, the situation as a way to practice self-talk. Do you want to play the role of your mom or yourself?

Cindy:	I'll be me!
Therapist:	Okay, I'll play the role of your mother. Do you want to start?
Cindy:	No way, you start!
Therapist:	(*laughs*) Okay: Cindy, where do you think you're going?
Cindy:	You know! Tonight is the all-night bowling party.
Therapist:	Oh no, you're not going to that party. I just found out there is no adult supervision! Why didn't you tell me that when you first asked to go?
Cindy:	How am I supposed to know? I didn't think about it, and you never asked. What's the big deal anyway? I'm fourteen, not a baby!
Therapist:	Well, maybe you'll think about it and tell me the full story next time. You can't go to this all-night bowling party.
Cindy:	I can't believe this—I'm all ready and everything. You never let me do anything! You always let Richie go everywhere. You treat me like a baby and I am sick of it.
Therapist:	Let's stop here. Good job, Cindy. Obviously, this was an upsetting situation for you. Let's identify and practice some good self-talk that you could use if a situation like this were to happen again. What could you have said that may have helped you not feel so bad?
Cindy:	I don't know. I was really mad. My mom really pisses me off. It was hard to think.
Therapist:	What could you have said that may have helped you not get as angry at your mom? Is it true that your mom never lets you go anywhere?
Cindy:	No. She usually is pretty cool. She lets me do a lot of things.
Therapist:	Okay. How about what you just said as some good self-talk?
Cindy:	Yeah. I could have reminded myself that Mom usually lets me do a lot of things, but maybe this was different since it was an all-nighter.
Therapist:	Is there a chance that she'll allow you to go to a future all-nighter, that has adult supervision?
Cindy:	Yeah. Probably. She'll say, "You can go if an adult is supervising."
Therapist:	So let's summarize some of the good self-talk that you could use in the future. Why don't you repeat some of the good self-talk that you could use.
Cindy:	"Mom isn't always on my case; she usually lets me do things and go a lot of places. It's probably because it's an all-nighter, and she'll be up all night worrying. She'll let me go next time if there are adults there."
Therapist:	Nice job. Sometimes when we're angry it's hard to think positively or rationally, but it's important for us to try, even if we have to wait a minute until we're more calm. Okay?
Cindy:	Yeah.

Feedback

Ask the child to clarify his or her understanding of the concepts presented during session.

Creative Experiment

Present the "Mr. & Ms. Feel Good Daily Rating Sheet." Instruct the child to fill out the sheet by rating his or her own feelings on a scale of one to ten. Also give the child "My Thoughts for Today" or "I Am Thinking" sheets to keep records of thoughts prior to the next session. These creative experiments can be used throughout the duration of treatment. "It's Like This . . ." and "I Have a Problem" can also be handed out to further explain the bad and good self-talk process.

Mr. & Ms. Feel Good Daily Rating Sheet

Name _____   Date _____   To _____

	Not at all Depressed								Very Depressed	
	1	2	3	4	5	6	7	8	9	10
MONDAY	☐	☐	☐	☐	☐	☐	☐	☐	☐	☐
TUESDAY	☐	☐	☐	☐	☐	☐	☐	☐	☐	☐
WEDNESDAY	☐	☐	☐	☐	☐	☐	☐	☐	☐	☐
THURSDAY	☐	☐	☐	☐	☐	☐	☐	☐	☐	☐
FRIDAY	☐	☐	☐	☐	☐	☐	☐	☐	☐	☐
SATURDAY	☐	☐	☐	☐	☐	☐	☐	☐	☐	☐
SUNDAY	☐	☐	☐	☐	☐	☐	☐	☐	☐	☐

Directions: Mark the box that corresponds with the number that best describes the severity of the depressed mood.

Mr. Feel Good

Ms. Feel Good

Mr. & Ms. Feel Good Daily Rating Sheet

Name _____   Date _____   To _____

	Not at all Depressed								Very Depressed	
	1	2	3	4	5	6	7	8	9	10
MONDAY	☐	☐	☐	☐	☐	☐	☐	☐	☐	☐
TUESDAY	☐	☐	☐	☐	☐	☐	☐	☐	☐	☐
WEDNESDAY	☐	☐	☐	☐	☐	☐	☐	☐	☐	☐
THURSDAY	☐	☐	☐	☐	☐	☐	☐	☐	☐	☐
FRIDAY	☐	☐	☐	☐	☐	☐	☐	☐	☐	☐
SATURDAY	☐	☐	☐	☐	☐	☐	☐	☐	☐	☐
SUNDAY	☐	☐	☐	☐	☐	☐	☐	☐	☐	☐

Mr. Feel Good

Ms. Feel Good

Directions: Mark the box that corresponds with the number that best describes the severity of the depressed mood.

My Thoughts for Today

Name _____

Date _____

Thought Diary

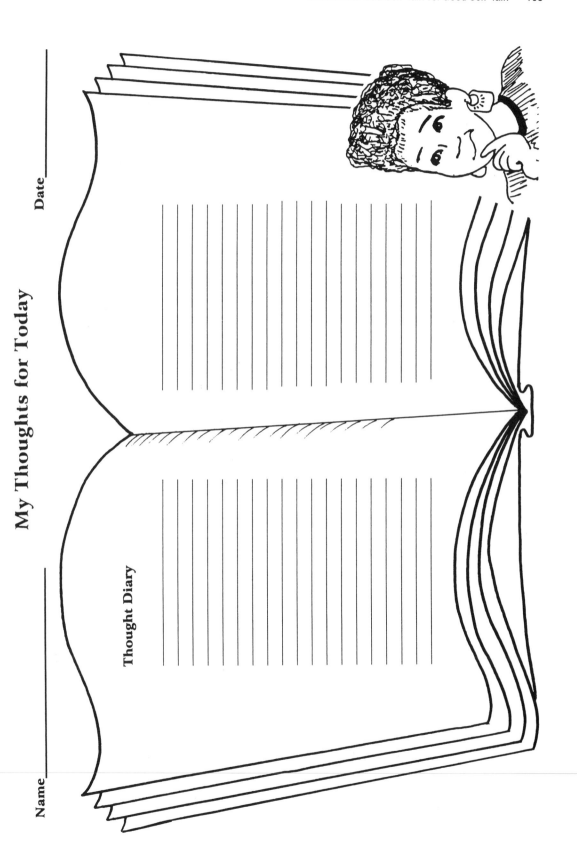

My Thoughts for Today

Name _____

Date _____

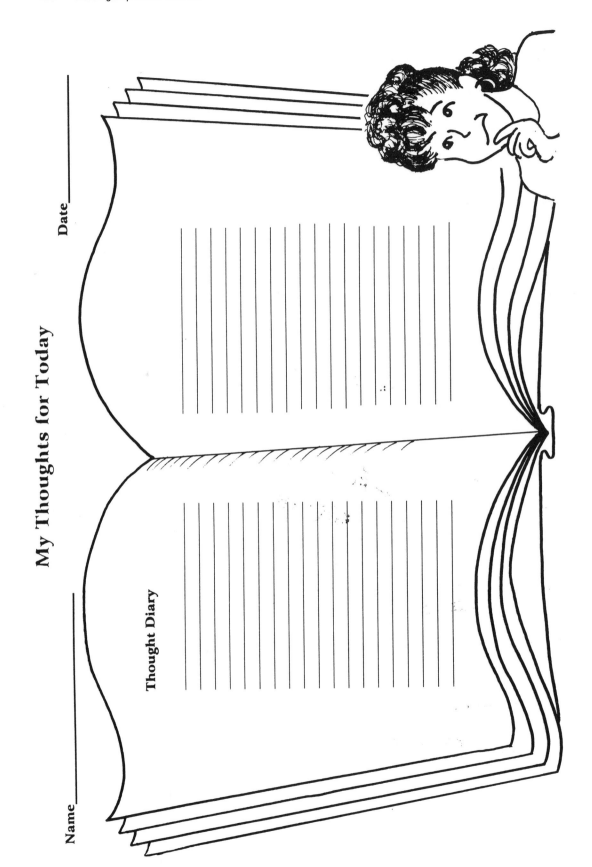

Thought Diary

I Am Thinking

Name_____   Date_____

My Thoughts Are...

_____

_____

_____

_____

_____

_____

_____

It's Like This

It's like this you see, I have this problem.

Because I had these thoughts like...

I started to feel...

I thought WHOA- take a chill - change those thoughts so I started to think...

After all that thinking I felt BETTER!!!

It's Like This

It's Like This

It's Like This

Because I had these thoughts like...

I started to feel...

After all that thinking I felt BETTER!!!

It's like this you see, I have this problem.

I thought WHOA- take a chill - change those thoughts so I started to think...

I Have a Problem

I have a problem

Automatic negative thoughts

Negative thoughts

Feelings

Get rid of those thoughts

Rational responses

I feel good

CHAPTER EIGHT

Session V:
Self-Esteem and Depression

*Objective: To teach the child about self-esteem
and how it affects behaviors and feelings*

Introduction

Briefly review the ABC Theory, rational responses (good self-talk), and the creative experiments from last session.

Agenda

- Define self-esteem.
- Elicit the child's perception of personality using the "Self-Esteem Word List" exercise.
- Discuss specific issues or concerns identified by the child.

Presentation/Exercise

Self-esteem is an important concept for all children and adults, regardless of cultural background, personality, interests, social experiences, abilities, and so on. Self-esteem can be defined as how a person sees himself or herself and how he or she is viewed by others in the environment. Positive self-esteem occurs when the child feels confident, appreciated, and understood for what he or she is. The depressed child often feels sad, worthless, and has many negative attitudes about himself or herself, usually due to negative life experiences. When a child has had painful or negative experiences, he or she often feels worthless.

Your task is to identify these traits of low self-esteem. For example, a child may dislike his or her appearance and state, "I'm fat, have frizzy hair, and freckles." The child may make derogatory statements such as, "I'm no good," "No one likes me," "I'm ugly," or "I'm dumb." Therefore, you need to help the child build, develop, or enhance self-esteem so he or she may feel good about himself or herself. When a child receives the message that he or she is a worthwhile human being, that he or she can cope with failures without feeling inadequate and worthless, self-esteem and a positive self-image can be achieved.

Ask the child to choose aspects of himself or herself that he or she dislikes and also aspects that he or she likes. If the child cannot identify these aspects, help the child come up with some ideas during the session.

Next, have the child create a list of words, both good and bad, taken from the "Self-Esteem Word List" that describes himself or herself. Encourage the child to express how he or she feels about each part of his or her own personality. Refer to the following example for further clarification:

Words That Describe Me	How I Feel About This Part of Me
1. Sad	1. I don't want my family to know I am sad.
2. Stupid	2. I feel that I should try harder because I am smart when I want to be.

After the child reviews the list, ask him or her to identify how others may see him or her. Children often do not realize that others may see them differently from how they actually see themselves.

At the end of the presentation, tell the child that children with positive self-esteem feel good about themselves and often accept responsibility for their own behaviors. Children with positive self-esteem also know good from bad; they can express thoughts and make good decisions about their own life and exhibit appropriate behaviors in home, school, or other social situations.

Feedback

Try to elicit thoughts and feelings from the child or adolescent about today's session.

Creative Experiment

Instruct the child to fill out the "Self-Esteem Sentence Completion" exercise using examples from his or her own life.

For Group Therapy

This exercise will give the children an opportunity to examine how they perceive themselves in comparison to how others see them.

Have children arrange chairs in a circle. Provide each child with five blank index cards and place a pile of blank index cards in the middle of the circle. Review with the children the "Self-Esteem Word List" displayed on the board by stating the words and defining terms that the children do not know or are unfamiliar with. Ask each child to select five words that describe him or herself and write each one on an index card. Instruct the child to look at each of the other group members for one to two minutes. Then ask the children to select from the "Self-Esteem Word List" one word that describes each group member and to write the word down on a blank index card taken from the pile in the middle of the circle. After everyone has finished writing their words, one by one instruct them to place the appropriate card face down on each group member's chair. Once this task is completed, each child should have two piles of cards; one pile contains cards that the child has written and the other contains cards that the other children have written. Ask the children to share the words they wrote about themselves, then the words that the group members wrote about them.

Encourage them to discuss their thoughts and feelings on how they perceive themselves as well as how they are perceived by others.

Self-Esteem Sentence Completion Exercise

Name_____   Date_____

1.   **I am fun to be with when** _____.

2.   **People like me because** _____.

3.   **I have accomplished** _____.

4.   **People respect me when** _____.

5.   **I like to** _____.

6.   **The best thing about me is** _____.

7.   **I feel great when I** _____.

8.   **I often dream about** _____.

9.   **When I grow up I want to** _____.

10.   **I feel important when I do** _____.

11.   **I am not ashamed to** _____.

12.   **I like people who** _____.

13.   **I know that I am** _____.

14.   **I believe** _____.

Self-Esteem Word List

Directions: Choose words from the following list to describe yourself.

Name_____   Date_____

angry	cheerful	greedy	mad
responsible	unsure	anxious	dumb
ignorant	obnoxious	sad	weird
active	depressed	intelligent	shy
playful	snobbish	withdrawn	bad
bully	dull	jealous	kind
perfect	silly	wild	bossy
disruptive	proud	emotional	lonely
patient	skinny	boring	fearful
liar	pleasant	tough	brainy
forgetful	lively	quiet	talkative
calm	fat	lovable	rude
tense	careful	good	mean
relaxed	ugly		

CHAPTER NINE

Session VI:
Joe Uses Good Self-Talk

---

*Objective: To help the child
identify automatic negative thoughts*

Introduction

Review basic concept of self-esteem and the creative experiment from last session.

Agenda

- o Introduce the "Child Thought Record."

- o Present the example of "Joe's Spelling Test."

- o Role-play problem situations.

- o Discuss any specific issues or concerns identified by the child.

Presentation/Exercise

Review ABC Theory concepts as well as rational response (good self-talk) concept. Hand out "Joe's Spelling Test" to demonstrate how to turn bad self-talk into good self-talk.

After Joe's example is provided, encourage the child to present a personal problem situation. The child's example should be presented using the "Child Thought Record."

During this session, role-play the situation with the child. Your primary goal is to elicit automatic negative thoughts from the child about his or her experiences. You can do this by helping the child reconstruct the event (that is, what happened) through role-playing. Ask questions, such as "What went through your head?" to elicit thoughts and feelings from the child about the situation or activating event. It is important to note that this process of teaching a child to identify automatic negative thoughts is not an easy task. Therapists who work exclusively with adults have reported a degree of difficulty teaching this skill during sessions; therefore, children will need additional support and guidance in order to identify automatic thoughts. Educating the child about identifying automatic negative thoughts is discussed in the following examples:

Therapist: Johnny, since you've been coming in to see me you've been learning a lot about good self-talk and bad self-talk. Most importantly, you have started to learn the connection between your thoughts and feelings. Remember that your thoughts are what you say to yourself. We've talked a lot about how important it is to change your negative thoughts, or bad self-talk, to more positive thoughts, or good self-talk. Today we are going to talk about how to catch up with and spot the bad self-talk so we can get rid of it and replace it with good self-talk.

Johnny: I know the difference between good self-talk and bad self-talk.

Therapist: Johnny, you catch on very fast. You've done quite well in picking out good self-talk and bad self-talk. However, it's very important to be able to spot bad self-talk as soon as these thoughts pop inside your head. Bad self-talk can also be referred to as automatic negative thoughts. Automatic thoughts are those thoughts that go through your head very quickly. Sometimes they occur so quickly that you can't catch up with them. However, when you slow your thoughts down, you can catch yourself, and then change your thoughts if they are bad or negative, to more realistic or positive thoughts. So do you think you understand what automatic thoughts are?

Johnny: I don't know.

Therapist: It'll probably be easier to explain what an automatic thought is by using an example. Johnny, can you think of any time during the past week when you felt upset about something?

Johnny: Umh . . . I kind of got yelled at by my teacher for forgetting my homework.

Therapist: What were you feeling when you realized that you forgot your homework and then got yelled at by your teacher?

Johnny: I don't know.

Therapist: Try to think very hard about that day at school. Try to picture inside your head what that day was like. Think about the classroom. Where were you? Were you standing or sitting? Who else was around you at the time? Most importantly, were you feeling angry, sad, afraid . . . ?

Johnny: I was sad and a little scared.

Therapist: Okay, Johnny, you were feeling sad and scared. Now remember that your emotions and feelings are caused by the self-talk that you use. This bad self-talk happens very quickly and pops into a child's head before he or she even realizes that the thought is there. These quick thoughts are the automatic thoughts. These automatic thoughts are usually the bad self-talk that we say to ourselves when a situation occurs that upsets us. So, when you forgot your homework, what thoughts quickly popped inside your head?

Johnny: I'm stupid.

Therapist: You just stated what is called an automatic negative thought. You said, "I'm stupid." This is also what we call . . . ?

Johnny: Bad self-talk.

Therapist: Johnny, it's very important for you to remember that bad self-talk are those automatic negative thoughts that quickly pop inside your head when something upsetting occurs. Everybody has automatic thoughts. Adults, like your parents and teachers, and also other kids experience these automatic thoughts. Most of the time we don't even pay any attention to these thoughts because they move very quickly through our heads. We realize that they are there when we begin to have different feelings. You know, all those feelings that we have talked about—fear, sadness, anger, and so on. Our feelings really let us know that we are having the automatic negative thoughts, or . . . ?

Johnny: Bad self-talk.

Therapist: You're absolutely correct. I also want you to learn that just because you have automatic thoughts, or bad self-talk, it doesn't mean those thoughts are true. Sometimes we believe our bad self-talk. That's why it's very important for you to be able to identify and catch your bad self-talk, or automatic thoughts. You said a little while ago that you were stupid when you forgot your homework. This was an automatic thought because it was probably one of the first things you said to yourself when the teacher yelled at you, right?

Johnny: Yeah.

Therapist: Well, just because this thought popped inside your head doesn't mean that it's true. I will be helping you learn how to push these automatic thoughts out of your head. Now let's take a close look at the automatic thought "I am stupid." How do you think you would feel if you said to yourself, "This isn't true, I know I'm not stupid."

Johnny: I wouldn't feel sad.

Therapist: You're probably right. I can bet that you'd probably feel a lot better. Let's take another look at the automatic thought "I am stupid." Did your teacher say "Johnny, you stupid boy, you forgot your homework"?

Johnny: No.

Therapist: She didn't call you stupid, but that sneaky automatic negative thought just flew right into your head and you said to yourself, "I am stupid."

Johnny: I'm not really stupid! I just forgot my homework, that's all.

Therapist: Good for you. All of us will forget something every now and then, but that doesn't mean that we are stupid. So when we begin to think like this we have to say to ourselves, "Hey, this isn't true, I'm not stupid." I have to say things to myself that will make me feel better. When I talk to myself in this way, what kind of self-talk am I using?

Johnny: Good self-talk.

Once again it is important to emphasize that eliciting automatic thoughts from a child can be a difficult task, but one that can be accomplished when you are creative and diligent in your approach of questioning the child about the problematic situation. When the child encounters difficulty verbalizing his or her account of the situation, gently coax the child to imagine the situation or reexperience the situation as if it were occurring in the here and now. In the above situation, the therapist could have introduced the role-playing technique if the child was unable to identify an automatic thought in an appropriate amount of time based on the therapist's judgment and relationship with the child.

If you work primarily with adolescents, refer to the following dialogue as an example of how to explain the automatic thought concept:

Therapist: Since you've been seeing me we've talked a lot about good and bad self-talk. We've also talked about the connection between your thoughts and feelings. Do you remember the difference between your thoughts and feelings?

Cindy: Yeah, my thoughts are what I say to myself; my feelings are how I feel, like sad or mad.

Therapist: Exactly! Today I thought we could spend some of our time talking about how to make sure you catch your negative, or automatic, thoughts when they occur. First, let's clarify what I mean by the term "automatic thoughts." Do you know what the term "automatic thoughts" means?

Cindy: I'm not sure . . . is it the same as bad self-talk?

Therapist: Yes, in many ways it is. Automatic thoughts are those thoughts that go through your head very quickly, before you really have a chance to think about them for any length of time. It's almost like these thoughts just automatically pop up in your head. Sometimes they occur so quickly that you can't even catch up with them. However, when we learn to slow our thoughts down, we can catch ourselves when we initially have the automatic thoughts.

Cindy: Why is this so important to learn how to do?

Therapist: Good question, Cindy. Automatic thoughts are often negative and inaccurate. Remember, automatic thoughts are quick to come into our heads and therefore are often inaccurate conclusions that we quickly make. Let's look closer at automatic thoughts by using an example. Can you think of any time during this past week when you felt upset about something?

Cindy: Oh yeah. My best friend really made me mad.

Therapist: What happened?

Cindy: Well, she and I always walk home together from school, but on Tuesday she accepted a ride home from some girl in our English class. They didn't even ask me if I wanted a ride!

Therapist: Think back and see if you can remember what your automatic thoughts were immediately after this happened, that is, what were the thoughts or self-talk that quickly popped into your head?

Cindy: She's a real jerk! Who does she think she is to treat me like this? I'll never speak to her again. She must be mad at me.

Therapist: Good job! You've just identified examples of automatic negative thoughts, which are the first thoughts that came into your head. How did you feel after having these thoughts?

Cindy: Mad! I also felt left out.

Therapist: Let's think back to your automatic thoughts. Now, when you look back do you believe your thoughts were accurate or correct? Is your friend really a jerk? Are you really never going to speak to her again?

Cindy: At the time I was really mad and the thoughts seemed correct. But now, I don't think so. I found out later that Amy was looking for me everywhere but couldn't find me. They waited for me, but finally had to leave because Shauna had to have the car home at exactly 3:30 P.M.

Therapist: So, in other words, your automatic thoughts—"Amy is a jerk," "She must be mad," and "I'll never speak to her again"—turned out to be incorrect.

Cindy: I guess so . . . Yeah.

Therapist: Cindy, it's important to know that everybody has automatic thoughts. Adults and kids experience these thoughts. Most of the time we don't pay attention to these thoughts, or we aren't even aware that we have them. This type of therapy, cognitive therapy, works to help teach us how to be aware of our automatic thoughts, then to evaluate the automatic thoughts to check if they are accurate, and finally, to learn how to replace the automatic negative thoughts with more realistic and accurate ones. Does this make sense?

Cindy: Yeah, it makes sense, but it sounds hard to do.

Therapist: You're right, at first it is rather difficult, but once you've practiced using accurate thinking or rational responses, it becomes much easier. Remember, the goal is for you to start using good self-talk. Now I want you to think back to last Tuesday when you found out that Amy got a ride home with Shauna. What other thoughts could you have had that would have helped you not feel as mad and upset?

Cindy: I don't know. I was real mad. I wanted to go off on her.

Therapist: I know you were feeling very angry. How do you think you would have felt if you said something like, "I can't believe she didn't wait on me, or even ask me to go, but I better wait and find out the whole story before I get too mad"?

Cindy: I would have still been upset, but not nearly as mad. That seems so easy when you say it.

Therapist: Exactly. I have had lots of practice and I also wasn't experiencing the feelings that you were, which makes it easier. But I think if you and I continue practicing, it will also become much easier for you. Remember, everybody has automatic thoughts; it's just important to become aware of our thoughts and how they affect our feelings, to evaluate them to see if they are true, and to learn to push the automatic thoughts away and replace them with more positive or realistic thoughts.

Helpful Strategies for Obtaining Automatic Thoughts

o Question the child about the problem situation.

o Ask the child what thoughts or pictures were going through his or her mind when the situation occurred.

o Role-play the actual event.

○ Utilize the "Daily Mood Calendar," "I Am Thinking," "Child Thought Record," or any other creative experiment to obtain automatic thoughts.

For Group Therapy

Ask for a volunteer to present his or her situation. You can also ask the children to break into smaller groups to role-play problem situations. Demonstrate the child's problem situation by using a chalkboard to further clarify these concepts.

Feedback

Try to elicit thoughts and feelings from the child or adolescent about today's session.

Creative Experiment

Give the child a "Child Thought Record" to complete for next session using his or her own personal problem situations.

Joe's Spelling Test

Name_____   Date_____

PROBLEM SITUATION: What were you doing when you started to feel BAD? What happened?	EMOTIONS: What feelings did you notice (sad, angry)? Rate them on a scale from one to ten.	AUTOMATIC THOUGHTS: What was going through your mind before you started to feel bad? BAD SELF TALK	RATIONAL RESPONSES: How could you handle the situation differently? GOOD SELF TALK	OUTCOME: How do you feel after you've tried to answer the thoughts in a more positive manner? Use a one to ten scale.
Joe earned a "D" grade on a spelling test.	1) Angry - 9 2) Sad - 10 3) Frustrated - 10	1) I'm stupid. 2) I always get failing grades. 3) My teacher doesn't like me.	1) I'm not stupid just because I got a "D" on a spelling test. I just need to study harder. 2) Hey! I don't always get failing grades. I have received "A's" before. 3) My teacher has been nice to me. She even told me not to worry.	1) I'll study harder next week. Angry - 2 Sad - 1 Frustrated - 1

Child Thought Record

Name_____

Date_____

PROBLEM SITUATION:	EMOTIONS:	AUTOMATIC THOUGHTS:	RATIONAL RESPONSES:	OUTCOME:
What were you doing when you started to feel BAD? What happened?	What feelings did you notice (sad, angry)? Rate them on a scale from one to ten .	What was going through your mind before you started to feel bad?	How could you handle the situation differently?	How do you feel after you've tried to answer the thoughts in a more positive manner? Use a one to ten scale.
		BAD SELF TALK	GOOD SELF TALK	

Session VII:
Destroy Bad Self-Talk

Objective: To help the child combat bad self-talk

Introduction

Begin the session with a brief review of last session, including collection and discussion of the creative experiment.

Agenda

- Review "Daily Mood Calendar" from session II.

- Review major objectives of cognitive therapy.

- Introduce "Enemy Camp vs. Enemy Destroyers" creative experiment, and for adolescents, the "Personal Problem-Solving Exercise."

- Discuss specific issues or concerns identified by the child.

Presentation/Exercise

Assess the child's compliance with the "Daily Mood Calendar" and review the child's perceptions of his or her overall mood. Emphasize the importance of daily compliance with this exercise, including the color key.

Present the "Enemy Camp vs. Enemy Destroyers" exercise, which is aimed at helping the child rid him or herself of automatic negative thoughts and cognitive distortions, as well as helping the child develop good self-talk (rational responses). This exercise is simple, concrete, and humorous; in it, cartoon characters are presented with the primary goal to "nuke" (destroy) negative thoughts that lead to depression. (**Note:** You must take on an active role during this exercise to dramatize the significance of these cartoon characters). Encourage the child to briefly describe a problem situation or upsetting event that may create conflict between negative automatic thoughts (bad self-talk) and positive rational responses (good self-talk).

The therapist in the following dialogue illustrates how to explain the "Enemy Camp vs. Enemy Destroyers" exercise to a child:

Therapist: Overall, it looks like you had a pretty good week, Johnny. You have filled out your "Daily Mood Calendar," and it shows that most of your days have been colored either green or yellow. (Green indicates a neutral mood and yellow is happy.) How is your mood right now?

Johnny: I don't know, okay I guess.

Therapist: Hmm . . . Something tells me that something is on your mind. Your facial expression is also telling me that maybe you have been using some bad self-talk. Am I correct?

Johnny: I don't know, maybe.

Therapist: Well, this exercise that I want to share with you today may help you think about the situation that might be bothering you. During the past few weeks, we have been doing a lot of talking about how our feelings and emotions are caused by our automatic thoughts. Remember, automatic thoughts are those thoughts that quickly pop inside your head when a problem situation occurs in your life. Johnny, do you recall having any automatic thoughts or bad self-talk today or anytime during the past week?

Johnny: I haven't been thinking too hard lately.

Therapist: Well, maybe this new exercise, called "Enemy Camp vs. Enemy Destroyers," will help you think a little bit about what may be bothering you. I may be wrong, but something tells me that something is bothering you.

Johnny: What are enemy destroyers?

Therapist: (*hands child a copy of the exercise*) Here, take a look. What do you think about the pictures?

Johnny: They're okay. Kind of funny.

Therapist: Johnny, what side do you think represents good self-talk and what side represents bad self-talk? Can you point them out for me.

Johnny: Oh, that's easy. The cartoon that looks like a little robot is the good person and the dragon is the bad enemy.

Therapist: (*laughs*) Hey, you're absolutely right.

Johnny: Where did you get this from?

Therapist: Do you mean where did I get the idea from?

Johnny: Yeah.

Therapist: Well, I know that kids your age like to play video games. It also seems that the purpose of a lot of video games is for the good guy to destroy the bad guy. Right?

Johnny: Yeah, but sometimes if you don't get enough points the bad guys will win and the good guys will lose.

Therapist: You're right, that does happen. However, this little robot on the good self-talk side, or what we can also refer to as the enemy destroyers' side, does not like to lose. He likes to win, and he does it by destroying bad self-talk. However, the bad self-talk side also likes to win. This dragon over here is pretty mean and vicious. He doesn't like to hear good self-talk. He likes kids to use bad self-talk. The enemy camp, where the dragon is big and powerful, is responsible for all those automatic negative thoughts that pop in a child's head when a problem situation comes up. This dragon doesn't care when a child begins to feel angry or sad, he just keeps firing out those automatic or negative thoughts. But the enemy destroyer camp, headed by the brave robot, is not afraid of the dragon and all the fire that comes out of his mouth, because he has powerful rays and beams that will wipe out and destroy any bad self-talk that tries to enter its territory. Johnny, do you understand the points I am trying to make?

Johnny: The robot is smiling.

Therapist: Why do you think he has a smile on his face?

Johnny: Because he's going to win the fight?

Therapist: The robot is already thinking good self-talk. He's not going to let the dragon invade his territory with bad self-talk. If he does, what do you think he'll do?

Johnny: He'll crush them. He'll send out his army of robots, right?

Therapist: The robot will do whatever it takes to destroy bad self-talk. Now let's take a closer look at this exercise. I'll read the directions: "Briefly describe problem or upsetting event that may create conflict (war) between automatic negative thoughts and positive rational responses." Johnny, can you think about a problem or something that may have upset you today that may have created a conflict, or war, between your good self-talk and bad self-talk?

Johnny: Well, I was mad when I got on the bus this morning.

Therapist: Did something happen before you got on the bus?

Johnny: No, not really.

Therapist: What was going on?

Johnny: I heard some kids talking about a birthday party that they went to on Saturday. When I got on the bus I asked my friend Bill what party they were talking about and he said it was Paula's. My friend went to the party and I wasn't invited.

Therapist: I see. Do you remember what automatic thoughts began to pop inside your head?

Johnny: No one likes me. I'm the only one who didn't get invited to the party.

Therapist: Okay, your automatic thoughts were "No one likes me," "I'm the only one who didn't get invited to the party." So are these thoughts coming from the enemy camp's side or the enemy destroyers' side?

Johnny: They are coming from the dragon's side. He's the enemy.

Therapist: So what must the robot and his enemy destroyers do?

Johnny: Nuke them and wipe them out.

Therapist: You got it, but now you must come up with some destroyer thoughts to get rid of the bad self-talk that you told yourself when you didn't get invited to the birthday party. The first thought that you mentioned was "No one likes me." Now what do you need to tell yourself to nuke this negative thought?

Johnny: Say, it's not true, I have friends.

Therapist: As a matter of fact, you already mentioned one friend.

Johnny: Yeah, my friend Bill.

Therapist: So instead of saying no one likes me, which is an automatic negative thought being fired from the dragon's enemy camp, you can fire right back with a positive thought from the enemy destroyers' side, and say, "Bill's my friend." Okay?

Johnny: Okay.

Therapist: Now let's talk about the other thought that you have to nuke. "I'm the only one who didn't get invited." What could you say to destroy this bad self-talk?

Johnny: Well, I'm not in the girl's class who had the party. I don't really know her.

Therapist: Okay, so you could say, "Maybe I wasn't invited because the girl barely knows me and I'm not in her class."

Johnny: She couldn't invite everybody.

Therapist: Good job, you're starting to wipe out the negative thoughts that you had. What else could you say to destroy the automatic thoughts coming from the enemy camp?

Johnny: I really didn't miss a whole lot. Bill said the party was at her house. They didn't even go to the arcade or Skate Land.

Therapist: Sounds like you didn't miss much. I guess most kids have parties at more interesting places.

Johnny: Yeah, house parties are boring. The last two parties I was invited to were at Skate Land.

Therapist: Johnny, I don't know if you're aware of what you've been saying, but you've said a few things that could easily wipe out the negative thoughts that you had when you found out that you were not invited to the party. You were kind of saying, "So what if I didn't get invited to the party, I don't really know the girl, I'm not in her class, I have friends, and the party was just at her house and not at a fun place like Skate Land." When you use this kind of self-talk who is winning the war? The dragon and the enemy camp or the robot with the enemy destroyers?

Johnny: The enemy destroyers, because they don't want me to talk bad about myself.

Therapist: You're right again, Johnny. Just remember that whenever you have a problem that comes about and you begin to feel angry or sad, it's the dragon firing those bad thoughts inside your head. When this happens, you have to get the robot prepared to destroy those thoughts by firing back with positive thoughts or good self-talk. When the robot does its job, you will most likely feel better than you did when the dragon was firing those thoughts that made you feel sad and angry. Let's finish this exercise by writing down your thoughts in the right columns. I'll give you an extra "Enemy Camp vs. Enemy Destroyers" exercise for you to do at home. This will be your creative experiment for next week, okay?

Johnny: Okay.

The above dialogue between the therapist and child is just another illustration that further explains how the child can learn to modify faulty thinking via use of a humorous or adventurous concept that the child can relate to.

For Group Therapy

Instruct the group to divide into two teams. One team will be the Enemy Camp and the other side will be the Enemy Destroyers. Describe in detail the purpose of the two teams utilizing the bad and good self-talk concepts. The Enemy Camp team will be responsible for coming up with bad self-talk and the Enemy Destroyers team will challenge the enemy with good self-talk. Ask the children to identify a problem or conflictual situation that may have occurred during the past week. After a situation is chosen by the group members, the Enemy Camp is given the opportunity to shout out examples of bad self-talk that may occur as a result of the conflictual situation. Then instruct the Enemy Destroyers team to challenge and destroy the bad self-talk by using examples of good self-talk. This exercise can be repeated by using other problem situations identified by the group participants.

Feedback

Try to elicit thoughts and feelings from the child about today's session.

Creative Experiment

Give the child a copy of the "Enemy Camp vs. Enemy Destroyers" exercise or the "Daily Mood Log" to complete for next session. Give adolescents the "Personal Problem-Solving Exercise" to complete.

Personal Problems Solving Exercise

Name _____   **Date** _____

I am feeling _____

_____

My problem is _____

_____

I am going to <u>stop and think</u> of as many solutions as I can, and think about their <u>consequence</u>.

_____

_____

Solutions I might try _____

_____

If I try it, what can happen next?

_____

_____

My plan for solving my problem is that I will

_____

_____

After I tried it and re-checked it, I found that it worked

_____

_____

and next time I might _____

_____

Source: Weisserg, R., Gesten, E., Liebenstein, N., Schmid, K.D.

Daily Mood Log

Name_____ **Date**_____

Describe problem situation or upsetting event:

_____
_____
_____
_____

Record feeling/emotion (rate each one from 0 (the least) to 10 (the most). Use words like angry, sad, anxious, afraid, etc.

Emotion: _____ **Rating:** _____   **Emotion:** _____ **Rating:**_____

Automatic/Negative Thoughts vs.	**Rational Responses**
Enemy Camp	**Enemy Destroyers**

_____   _____

_____   _____

_____   _____

_____   _____

_____   _____

_____   _____

_____   _____

_____   _____

Enemy Camp vs. Enemy Destroyers

Name _____   Date _____

Problem Situation

Briefly describe problem or upsetting event that may create conflict (war) between automatic negative thoughts and positive rational responses:

Enemy Camp
Automatic *NEGATIVE* thoughts
BAD

vs

Enemy Destroyers
Rational *POSITIVE* thoughts
GOOD

EMOTION: Record your feeling and rate on a scale from 0 (least) to 10 (most) (sad, angry, afraid, mad, lonely, anxious and so on)

Emotion _____   Number _____

OUTCOME: Review ENEMY DESTROYER rational responses and check the box that describes how you feel

Better ☐   somewhat better ☐   not at all better ☐

CHAPTER ELEVEN

Session VIII:
Stress and Steps to Relax

---

*Objective: To explain the effects of
stress and how to relieve it*

Introduction

Begin the session with a brief review of last session, including the creative experiment.

Agenda

o Review automatic negative thoughts (bad self-talk) vs. rational responses (good self-talk).

o Define *stress*.

o Present relaxation training and techniques aimed at targeting stress and depressive symptoms.

o Discuss specific issues or concerns identified by the child.

Presentation/Exercise

A child often hears about stress on the radio or television, but you should make sure that he or she really understands what it is before continuing. As long as someone is alive, he or she will always experience some type of stress, whether it is small (getting up to go to school) or is perceived to be rather large (big test in a difficult class or auditioning for a play). Stress is caused by a variety of things. Most often it occurs when a person has too many things on his or her mind (worrying), too many things to do, or conflicts and arguments with others. In other words, stress occurs when someone is under pressure from too many demands. Too much stress in a person's life can lead him or her to feel out of control.

A child, like an adult, can often experience physical symptoms when under stress. Physical symptoms are very important and often serve as warnings that too much stress is occurring. For example, when a person is under too much stress, he or she may experience rapid heartbeat, headaches, and stomachaches. Other messages that indicate stress can include eating too quickly, impatience, talking too fast, having difficulty relaxing and having fun, having trouble concentrating, and feeling cranky. Emotional reactions are also present during stressful situations, and the most common feeling is anger. Sometimes when a person is angry, he or she yells, screams, throws things, and becomes very frustrated. Therefore, it is very important to learn how to handle stress and manage anger. Before specific ways to handle stress are presented, review the following items that are commonly stressful for children:

o Fear of being disliked by others

o Desire to be the best in everything

o Desire to win

o Desire to be perfect

o Fear of failing in school

o Desire to be first in everything

o Fear of not having fun during activities

o Waiting in line

When these behaviors occur or sound familiar to the child, emphasize that relaxation may help reduce or stop these behaviors.

Relaxation training has also been used to treat symptoms of depression. Why? Because low self-esteem and anxiety are most often associated with depressed mood, and relaxation training has been found to reduce these symptoms (Reynolds and Coats 1986). Provide a brief explanation of relaxation training and demonstrate some techniques. Explain that the primary objective of relaxation training is for the child to understand the relationship between stress, muscle tension, and depression, and also to learn specific skills to facilitate self-relaxation.

Progressive Relaxation

Teach the child to relax various major muscle groups using the steps indicated below. You may want to refer to specific procedures outlined by Bernstein and Borkovec (1973) in their book, *Progressive Relaxation—A Manual for Therapists*.

Before you begin, remind the child to follow these suggestions when relaxing on his or her own:

o Choose a quiet room where there are few distractions.

o Choose a time of day when you are least likely to be disturbed by others.

o Choose a positive word or phrase to repeat silently or aloud while you practice your relaxation exercises. Choose a word that is pleasing to you.

o Select a comfortable position. Sit in a comfortable position on your bed or in a soft, comfortable chair. Try not to fall asleep while relaxing.

When you are sure that the child is comfortable and has chosen a positive word or phrase, take him or her through the following relaxation procedures:

Note: It is important to talk in a quiet, soothing voice.

1. Sit quietly in a comfortable position.

2. Close your eyes.

3. Relax all of your muscles as fully and deeply as possible. Start with front leg muscles, and one group at a time, lead up to your facial muscles, or start with your facial muscles and work your way down.

4. Breathe naturally. As you breathe out, say your favorite word or phrase.

5. Continue this exercise for fifteen to twenty minutes. When you finish, sit quietly and think of a positive, relaxing scene.

Recommend that the child practice this method for fifteen to twenty minutes, once or twice per day, preferably at a regularly scheduled time and place. The following dialogue illustrates a brief excerpt of a therapist introducing a child to relaxation exercises. You can assist the child, when appropriate, through demonstrating the techniques.

Therapist: As I just stated, stress occurs in everyone's life. Can you tell me what kind of situations cause you to feel stressed out?

Child: When teachers give me too much homework, or when I have to study for a big test.

Therapist: A lot of kids feel stressed out by schoolwork. It's very common for kids to sometimes feel worried and anxious about doing well in school.

Child: Sometimes I get angry and upset when I have a lot of homework.

Therapist: Anger is a very common feeling or emotion to have when a person is under stress. Can you think of any other situations that have caused you to experience stress in the past?

Child: I had to give a book report in my science class two weeks ago.

Therapist: Yes, I do remember you talking a little bit about your presentation.

Child: Yeah, I was nervous and thought I was going to mess up.

Therapist: Although you were feeling anxious and nervous, you did well. During that session we practiced using good self-talk.

Child: It helped me a little bit. I wasn't as nervous as I thought I would be.

Therapist: Well, relaxation exercises are something you can use, as well as good self-talk, when you're feeling stressed out, upset, nervous, anxious, or angry about some-thing that is occurring in your life. You can also practice relaxation when you are feeling down and depressed, or when your self-esteem is low. Your mus-cles become very tense when you experience stressful situations that bring about nervous, angry, and depressed feelings. So when you do relaxation ex-ercises, your whole body is involved. You may want to refer to relaxation as special exercises, or creative experiments, that will make you feel good inside.

I'm going to take you through the relaxation steps so that you can practice later, okay?

Child: Okay.

Therapist: The first step in this exercise is for you to sit comfortably in your chair. When you do these relaxation exercises at home, choose your favorite chair. Some kids prefer to lie down on their bed. Okay, try to make yourself as comfortable as possible. Keep your feet firmly on the floor and put your hands at your side. (*Therapist models techniques for the child during this training period.*) I want you to concentrate very hard as I tell you what to do. Now we get to deep breathing. Take a deep breath in through your nose ... and let it out through your mouth, like this (*Therapist demonstrates proper breathing*). Very good ... Now I want you to close your eyes slowly ... Take another deep breath in through your nose and let it out through your mouth slowly. Now I want you to think of a pleasant or happy picture or scene, something that makes you feel very relaxed and good inside. You can also pretend or imagine that you are very far away in a magical land or on a beautiful island. You can be anywhere you want. Let your body relax as you think of this beautiful, quiet place or picture. Continue to breathe slowly in and out ... Good job. (*Therapist counts for thirty to sixty seconds as the child is encouraged to imagine this scene.*) Now I want you to focus your attention on your face. Your facial muscles are very important. I want you to tighten your face muscles by scrunching your eyes together. Pretend that you are frowning or making a face. Can you feel your facial muscles becoming tense?

Child: (*nods*) Yeah.

Therapist: Very good. Now relax them. Get rid of the frown. Let your cheeks and jaw relax. Allow all your facial muscles to relax. Let your lips and chin relax. Can you feel the difference when your face muscles are relaxed? Now I want you to breathe slowly, in and out. Next we will move on to your hands and arms. Clench your hands together and make a tight fist. Also tighten up your arms. Feel the tight feelings in your hand and arm muscles. Now relax them and let them go limp ...

Continue to direct the child to focus his or her attention on different muscles. It is important for the child to first tighten each muscle and then relax the muscle. Closely monitor the child for appropriate breathing as well as tensing up and relaxing the appropriate muscles. Demonstrating these relaxation exercises in the child's presence will decrease noncompliance. Children will often verbalize feeling uncomfortable when asked to practice these techniques in the presence of the therapist. However, I've found that they will agree to engage in relaxation once they are appropriately educated about the purpose for practicing these techniques. Children tend to feel more comfortable when the therapist also practices the exercises simultaneously. Noncompliance usually occurs outside of the therapy session. Adolescents in particular should not be forced to practice these techniques. Remember that when adolescents believe something is good for them, they definitely won't do it. One way to address noncompliance is to bring the issue up during the session in a matter-of-fact manner. Ask what was going on that prevented them from practicing the techniques. Oftentimes the adolescent may not have understood the rationale behind the exercises, therefore more psychoeducation may be necessary.

Younger children will most likely need to be prompted by parents to engage in the techniques when they experience stressful situations. Parents will of course need to be made aware of what their role will be. In my experience as a therapist, I have instructed parents of younger children to prompt them to practice these relaxation techniques at specific times of the day. Parents should be supportive and coax children, but as was emphasized earlier, do not pressure them since this will most likely increase noncompliance and resistance.

Providing praise on a consistent basis has also been determined to be effective in reducing noncompliance to relaxation exercises. Praise reinforces success, which is an effective method of learning. When children report during a therapy session that they have not utilized the relaxation exercises, you may consider taking the child through the relaxation process again; this may also decrease noncompliance. Refer to the following dialogue in which the therapist is not deterred when the child reports not practicing the exercises that were introduced during a previous session:

Therapist: You have been talking a little bit about having a difficult week and I wonder if you were able to use any of the relaxation exercises that were introduced to you last time you were here?

Child: Not really.

Therapist: Did you try any of the breathing techniques or practice tensing and relaxing different muscles?

Child: No. I didn't think much about it. I didn't really have any big problems.

Therapist: Well, you don't need to have "big problems" to use relaxation exercises, but let's talk about why relaxation is important. Do you remember what important things we talked about last week?

Child: You told me about stress. When you feel stressed out about things or feel nervous you can practice relaxation.

Therapist: Yes, you're correct. We also talked about the relationship between problem situations, negative thinking, upset feelings, and how they all contribute to stress. Relaxation exercises can be helpful because they can help a person feel better inside. Do you remember how you felt last week when I took you through the exercises?

Child: Yeah, I felt pretty good. I almost fell asleep.

Therapist: Sounds like you were almost too relaxed.

Child: I guess so.

Therapist: Relaxation exercises can be very helpful as I explained to you before; however, it's up to you whether or not you practice them. I can encourage you to try these exercises, but I'm not at home with you to make sure that you practice them when you feel stressed, upset, or angry. It'll be your decision to do the exercises, although I believe that they'll help you feel better when problem situations occur. I also want to add that you can use these exercises at any time, even when you are not experiencing problems or difficult situations.

Child: Well, I couldn't remember all the steps.

Therapist: How about if I take you through the steps again and then write them down for you? Would that help you out?

Child: I guess so.

Therapist: I also have a relaxation tape that I'll share with you today that takes you through the steps. The music in the background is very comforting. The person on the tape has a very soft, calming voice that will help you relax as she tells you what muscles or body parts to focus on. The tape may help you remember the steps. Would you like to try the tape?

Child: Okay.

Therapist: I don't want you to feel pressured to do the exercises, although they can be very helpful. After we practice the steps during the session, I want you to give the tape a try and you can let me know next week how you did, okay?

Child: Okay.

It is important to note that the child may not practice relaxation exercises even though they have been educated about the importance of utilizing these techniques to reduce symptoms of depression and anxiety. As was indicated previously, parents can monitor or gently coax the child to practice relaxation, but badgering or forcing the child will most likely increase resistance and noncompliance. Try to address the issue in a matter-of-fact manner during the session and then engage the child in the techniques during the session.

After the child has practiced relaxation steps for a few weeks, he or she may be able to use this method when in a stressful or tension-producing situation. You may also suggest the following as quick relaxation tips:

o Take a deep breath and focus on your breathing for a few minutes.

o Say a special word and picture yourself relaxing in your favorite place.

o Relax the muscles or the part of your body that feels the most tense.

Feedback

After the relaxation exercise is completed, encourage the child to report if he or she has experienced any physical or emotional changes. Try to elicit thoughts and feelings from the child about today's session.

Creative Experiment

Introduce the "Daily Monitoring" relaxation exercise sheet. Instruct the child to complete the exercise for the next session.

For Group Therapy

The following exercise, Mill Around and Shake Off Stress, can be used as a group relaxation warm-up exercise:

Instruct the children to stand and take a big stretch (arms above head, on tiptoe, and so on) and then to drop their arms. Then instruct them to bend over at the waist and walk around the room, swinging their arms back and forth, pretending to shake off stress, worries, problems, and so on. For example, you can say, "Shake off your worry about the upcoming test, shake off the stress of wanting to get all As, shake off the stress that you didn't get picked for the class play." Encourage the children to shout out any stressful experiences or situations and to pretend to shake them off. This is a fun group experience that promotes laughter and releases tension and anxiety.

The next exercise can be used after the warm-up to help children learn to relax their bodies by tensing and relaxing muscles.

Instruct the children to find a comfortable spot on the floor and lie down. Mats should be provided for hard floors. Using a calm, soothing voice, give the following instructions (**Note:** Pause five to ten seconds after each instruction):

Children, now we're going to let our whole body relax. Try to get as comfortable as you can. We will go through different parts of the body, telling each part to relax. Now let your attention go to your toes. Squeeze your toes tightly . . . and let them relax. Tighten the muscles in your feet . . . now relax them. Squeeze your legs together . . . tell them to relax. Clench your hands together and ball them into a fist . . . tell them to relax. Tighten the muscles in your arms . . . tell them to relax. Tighten your stomach muscles . . . tell them to relax. Squeeze your shoulders together . . . tell them to relax. Tighten your neck muscles . . . tell them to relax. Scrunch your face muscles . . . make an ugly frown . . . now make a big smile . . . tell your face muscles to relax . . . tell your mouth to relax. Now just lie completely still and relax . . . breathing slowly in and out. Think about something pleasant or something you enjoy doing that's quiet and

For Group Therapy
(continued)

relaxing. Continue to think about this pleasant thing for about two minutes (pause for two minutes). When I begin to count to ten, I want you to begin to let your body become alive again. When I reach ten you will feel relaxed and alert and slowly get up ... 1-2-3-4-5-6-7-8-9-10. Slowly get up and take a seat.

After this exercise is completed, the children are asked to share their personal experiences about the exercise (thoughts, visual images, physical sensations).

Daily Monitoring: Relaxation in Problem Situations

Name _____

Date _____

DAY OF WEEK	PROBLEM SITUATION	SCALE: 0-10
SUNDAY		
MONDAY		
TUESDAY		
WEDNESDAY		
THURSDAY		
FRIDAY		
SATURDAY		

Scale: 0 = Most Relaxed
          10 = Most Tense

CHAPTER TWELVE

Session IX:
Stress, Anger, and Relaxation

Objective: To teach the child about the relationship between stress and anger and how relaxation can be used to ease both

Introduction

Briefly review the last session, including the "Daily Monitoring" relaxation exercise sheet.

Agenda

- Review relaxation procedures.
- Utilize a relaxation tape.
- Role-play anger- or stress-producing situations.
- Discuss specific issues or concerns identified by the child.

Presentation/Exercise

Introduce anger- or stress-producing hypothetical situations to be enacted (that is, role-played) during session. Refer to the "Stressed and Angry" exercise for situations. These scenarios have been created in order to arouse emotional feelings in the child and to demonstrate how self-assertive responses and good self-talk reduce stress and anger. After each situation has been role-played, review the relaxation procedures first introduced in session VIII.

Guide the child through the relaxation procedures from session VIII as a warm-up to the relaxation tape.

Instruct the child to take a comfortable position in the room. Dim the lights and turn on the tape for about fifteen minutes.

For Group Therapy

Encourage children to position themselves four or five feet apart from each other to facilitate maximum relaxation benefits. After the group completes the relaxation techniques, engage the participants in a discussion about their feelings and responses to the exercise.

Feedback

Try to elicit the child's thoughts and feelings following this exercise. Then ask the child to compare current feelings (perceptions) as well as feelings experienced prior to the relaxation tape.

Creative Experiment

Instruct the child to practice relaxation procedures at least two times prior to the next session, particularly when faced with a stress-producing situation.

Stressed and Angry

Directions: Read the following situations that may evoke feelings of anger and other stress-related symptoms.

1. Jim is trying to finish a chemistry project, however his sister is listening to the stereo so loud that he can't concentrate.

2. Jill's best friend, Tonya, has been hanging around with a group of kids who frequently party, skip school, and recently started drinking and using drugs. Tonya just asked Jill to attend a party with the crowd. Jill likes Tonya, but doesn't want to get involved.

3. Mr. Williams has several dogs and never keeps them in the house or tied up. For the past few days, one of the dogs has been using your yard as the "neighborhood toilet" and your mother has been making you clean up the mess.

4. Tom is the neighborhood jokester. He is very silly, but often makes rude remarks about people. Yesterday he began making fun of your mother's weight problem, but you ignored it and walked away. Well today, he started up again by saying, "How's the hippo?"

5. Your father decides that you need a haircut and suggests that you get a crew cut. You want a style that is fashionable, however, because you don't want to be the oddball at school.

CHAPTER THIRTEEN

Session X:
Learning Social Skills

*Objective: To teach the child about appropriate
social skills and how and when to use them*

Introduction

Begin the session with a brief review of the relaxation procedures presented during the last session and discuss the child's ability to utilize these relaxation procedures.

Agenda

- Introduce social skills.
- Demonstrate appropriate social skills and encourage the child to role-play these skills during interpersonal situations.
- Discuss specific issues or concerns identified by the child.

Presentation/Exercise

Social skills refers to an individual's ability to relate to other people in a positive, effective, and productive manner, which is very important in our society. A child learns social skills by first being introduced to the skills and situations in which they should be used. The most effective way to do this is through structured exercises and role-playing. It's important to stress that social skills are not innate; a child is not born with social skills, he or she has to learn them.

Prior to educating the child about each particular social skill, you should first assess the child's baseline knowledge of the skill. A clinical interview is the most common assessment technique, although most therapists are aware that the majority of clinical interviews are not standardized and tend to be subjective. Despite these limitations, it is crucial to determine if the child is deficient in a particular skill. You may begin this process by asking the child each time a skill is introduced if he or she has some understanding or knowledge of it. If the child acknowledges familiarity with the particular skill, ask the child to describe his or her understanding of the skill. If the child exhibits the ability to successfully verbalize or demonstrate his or her knowledge of the skill, you will not need to spend time educating the child about the skill. Not every child will need to learn all social skills during the course of treatment. For example, some children who appropriately maintain eye contact when they are spoken to may not need to be educated at length about the importance of appropriate eye contact. The child who displays a particular social skill in an acceptable manner should be praised and given feedback that he or she is already using the skill successfully. Referring back to the eye contact social skill for example, the therapist may say to the child, "We won't need to spend much time at all discussing appropriate eye contact because you do a very nice job looking at me when we talk. When you do this, it shows me that you are listening to me and are interested in what I am saying, etc."

As was indicated previously, it is essential to first establish a baseline of the child's social skills deficit. It's also important to note that educating the child about each skill will require more time than is indicated for one session. You may need to devote several sessions to adequately teaching the child social skills, particularly those children who exhibit severe social skills deficits. You should first briefly describe each of the following social skills:

Eye Contact. Appropriate eye contact is a very important social skill. It's important to teach children that eyes are not only used for seeing, but are also important for communicating, interacting, and listening to others. Looking at people when you talk to them shows them that you are listening and paying attention to what is being said. Appropriate eye contact can also be defined as looking at others consistently, with some breaks in between, during interactions. Be sure to stress that staring, however, should be avoided.

The child should also be taught that eye contact avoidance occurs when the person looks down at the floor or looks around the room the majority of the time during interactions with others. When teaching the child about the importance of establishing good eye contact, you should stress that looking at someone when he or she is talking shows that you are interested in what is being said. The following dialogue can be initiated once you have educated the child about appropriate eye contact:

Therapist: Can you tell me why appropriate eye contact is important when you talk or interact with others?

Child: You need to look at people.

Therapist: Right! Our eyes are very important for seeing and looking. Making eye contact lets a person know that you are interested in what is being said. What would you think if I started staring at you like this (*therapist stares*) while we were talking?

Child: You look silly.

Therapist: I also feel silly when I stare. How do you feel when someone looks at you for a long period of time?

Child: I don't like it.

Therapist: Staring at people can make them feel uncomfortable. Staring is also not appropriate eye contact. It's important to look at people when we talk; however, it's not appropriate to stare at people for long periods of time without looking away briefly. Tell me if you think I am giving you appropriate eye contact now (*therapist looks down at the floor*), if I talk with you for the next several minutes with my head down.

Child: No. You aren't looking at me.

Therapist: If you look down at the floor or at your shoes when someone is talking to you or when you're talking to someone, you are not practicing good eye contact.

You may want to role-play the following situations to further educate the child about appropriate eye contact:

o You're watching television at home and your mother asks you to clean your room. Using your eyes, show me what you would do.

o A friend is talking to you about a book that he or she just read that is very good. What are you doing when your friend is talking?

o You're drawing at your desk during recess, and your teacher comes into the room and announces that class is about to start. Where should you look and what should you do?

Personal Distance (Appropriate Personal Space). Appropriate personal space may be described to children as "right space," because this concept is easier to understand. Space, or proximity, is the distance between the child and another person. Children should be informed that it's important to respect a person's personal space. If a person is too close, or too far away, problems are likely to occur when trying to talk to him or her. You can tell the child that the right space is an arm's length away. To demonstrate this social skill, you may want to refer to the following dialogue:

Therapist: Right space is a very important skill to remember when talking or interacting with people, both adults and children. Right space basically means being not too close or not too far away when you're talking with someone. Right space is the right distance between you and the other person. I'll show you what I mean. (*Therapist stands and directs the child to stand also.*) Let's pretend we are standing in line at the movie theater or amusement park. I want you to pretend that there is a person standing in front of you, and I'll pretend to be another person standing behind you. I'm going to act like I'm really excited and anxious to get inside. (*Therapist stands close to the child, leaving minimal space between them.*) Is this appropriate personal distance or right space?

Child: No! I don't have any room (*laughs*).

Therapist: You're absolutely right! How does it make you feel when someone is standing so close that you can't stretch out your arm?

Child: I don't like it. I feel like I'm being squeezed in.

Therapist: When other people don't give you right space you can feel squeezed in or closed in. The most important thing that you must remember about right space is being able to extend or stretch one arm in front of you and the other arm behind you. (*Therapist demonstrates this skill.*) Now I want you to show me right space.

After the child has appropriately demonstrated this skill, you may conclude by stating, "If you can't extend or stretch out your arm, or if you bump or brush against the person, then you don't have right space.

You may also want to engage the child in a role-playing activity to increase his or her understanding of the "right space" concept. The following scenarios may be used:

o You are standing in line in the school cafeteria. How far from or how close should you be to the person in front of you?

o You need to ask your teacher a question and you walk over while he or she is standing at the blackboard. How far away or close should you be standing?

o You are about to ask your friend to borrow a game that he or she is playing with. How close or far away should you stand?

Once the child is capable of demonstrating his or her understanding of the social skill via role-plays, the therapist can move on to another skill.

Appropriate Voice Tone. How a person talks to another person is very important. Children need to be educated about how to distinguish and understand the difference between appropriate and inappropriate use of voice volume. An "indoor voice" should be used when talking quietly in a library; an "outdoor voice" can be used for cheering on a sports team. Voice tone is also important because it allows a person to express feelings clearly so that other people can understand them. It is important to emphasize that people use special voices for different situations. The following dialogue clearly shows how the voice tone social skill can be explained to a child:

Therapist: Using appropriate voice tone, or your "right voice," is very important when you talk to people. Our voices can help us express our feelings and let people know how we feel in different situations. Children, as well as adults, have a special voice for different situations. There are times when we talk loudly and there are times when we talk quietly. There are also times when we talk in a regular voice. I'm going to practice different voices for you and I want you to tell me if I'm using the right voice for the situation, okay?

Child: Okay.

Therapist: I'm pretending to be outside at a relay race at school. I'm cheering for my team. I start to say (*therapist whispers*), "Run, run." Is this the right voice to cheer my friends on?

Child: No one will hear you.

Therapist: Okay. If I use a louder voice and yell (*therapist demonstrates by using louder voice tone*), "Run, run," is this an appropriate voice for the relay race?

Child: (*laughs*) Yeah, you were loud.

Therapist: Should I use this same voice in the library, if I need to ask the librarian to help me find a book?

Child: No. You might get in trouble if you yell in the library.

Therapist: You're right. Now, I want you to show me what voice you would use if you needed to ask the librarian a question.

Child: I would talk very softly.

Therapist: Okay, but I want you to practice using your soft voice. Why don't you say, in a soft voice, "I need help finding a book."

Child: (*softly*) "I need help finding a book."

Therapist: Good job. Now I'm going to give you a little quiz and I want you to tell me if you should use a soft voice, loud voice, or a regular voice, okay? Now for your first quiz question: You're over at your friend's house and you're talking about a movie you just saw. What type of voice should you use?

Child: A regular voice?

Therapist: Correct. A regular voice is the right voice for this situation. Okay, second quiz question: You are at the movie theater and the movie has just started. You want to ask your friend to pass the popcorn and candy. What type of voice would you use?

Child: I'd whisper or talk in a soft voice.

Therapist: Good answer. Talking in a whisper or using a soft voice is the right voice when you are watching a movie.

The therapist can continue to provide different examples and also utilize the role-playing technique to further educate the child about the appropriate use of this social skill.

Greetings. Greetings, or "openers," are words or statements that start conversations or interactions with others. Greetings are simple things to say when a person is interested in getting someone's attention, and are particularly useful in helping a person get to know new people. An appropriate opener can be as simple as "Hello, my name is . . . What's yours?" During the session in which this social skill is presented, you should demonstrate appropriate "openers" through role-playing. The following dialogue can be used as a guideline:

Therapist: I just gave you a few examples of "openers" or greetings, that we use when we want to start a conversation with a person. Can you give me an example of another appropriate "opener"?

Child: "Hi, how are you?"

Therapist: Very good! Now I want you to tell me if this is an example of a positive or an appropriate greeting? "Hey you."

Child: No, you didn't say hi or hello first.

Therapist: You're right. How about this greeting? "Who are you?"

Child: You still didn't say hello.

Therapist: Correct. It is very important to remember that you don't start conversations or begin talking to people with comments or statements like "Hey you," or "Who are you?" How about this one? "How are you doing?"

Child: It's okay.

Therapist: You're right again. Let's do some quick role-playing. I'll pretend that I'm in your art class and you want to borrow my paints. You come over to me while I am painting a picture and start to talk to me, okay?

Child: Okay.

Therapist: Let's start.

Child: Excuse me. Can I borrow your paints?

Therapist: Yes, you can. Why don't you sit down and paint with me?

Child: Okay.

Therapist: Good job! Let's do another one. I'll pretend that I'm the new child at school and I sit next to you in class. Tell me what you might say.

Child: Hi, my name is . . . . What's yours?

Therapist: Good opener!

You should continue with similar examples until the child has fully grasped this social skill.

The last two social skills to be introduced are good listening and nonverbal communication. These skills are higher level social skills because they incorporate skills previously learned or identified. In order to effectively teach these skills to a child, you must be certain that the child has fully grasped the more basic skills (eye contact, voice tone, personal space, and greetings).

Good Listening. Listening is a very important social skill and perhaps one of the most difficult to explain to children. Teaching this skill can be more effective when you role-play, or model, appropriate and inappropriate listening behaviors for the child. Children are initially informed that listening involves hearing and the use of one's ears. However, to listen effectively one is required to make use of his or her entire body. Children need to be reminded that good listening involves paying attention to what is being said by another person. Good listening skills can also promote peer interactions. In the following dialogue, the therapist will discuss the importance of the relationship between listening and previously learned social skills:

Therapist: Good listening is one of the most important social skills you will learn about. When you talk with a friend or an adult you need to pay attention, use good eye contact, use your right voice, and also make sure that you maintain or keep appropriate personal distance, or "right space." You already know that your ears allow you to listen, but your eyes are also important. Do you remember why?

Child: You have to look at people when you are talking.

Therapist: Right. If I don't look at a person when I am talking, the person may think that I'm ignoring him or her or am not interested in what he or she is saying. Would you think that I'm a good listener if I started watching television and was talking to you at the same time?

Child: No.

Therapist: It's very difficult to try to do two things at once. If I was talking to you and watching television at the same time, I would miss out on many of the things you were talking about. Let's try more role-playing.

Child: Okay.

Therapist: Why don't we stick with the television situation. I want you to pretend to be watching television and the volume is up. I want to talk with you so I will ask you to turn the volume down. I want you to use poor listening skills. In other words, I don't want you to listen, okay?

Child: Okay.

Therapist: Let's start now. Pretend that you are really into your television program: Excuse me, would you mind turning down the volume? (*Child ignores question.*) Hello, did you hear me? I would really like you to turn down the volume so we can talk.

Child: (*laughs and continues to look straight ahead*)

Therapist: (*using louder voice tone*) I'm asking you a question. Would you please turn down the volume? (*When the child continues to ignore requests, the therapist pretends to turn the television off.*)

Child: Hey, what are you doing?

Therapist: Didn't you hear me talking to you?

Child: No. I was watching my favorite show.

Therapist: Good job. Now let's talk about what happened. Were you using good listening skills?

Child: No. I was ignoring you.

Therapist: In what way were you ignoring me?

Child: Well, I didn't answer when you asked me to turn the TV down.

Therapist: Okay. How else did you show poor listening?

Child: I didn't look at you while you were talking.

Therapist: Exactly. You never made any eye contact. You just looked straight ahead at the television. You also failed to follow directions.

Child: Yeah . . . I didn't turn the television down when you asked me to.

Therapist: Good listeners pay attention, make good eye contact, and follow directions. Although you were in the right space and not too far away from me, you still showed poor listening skills. If you were to show me good listening skills, what would you do differently?

Child: I would answer you and turn down the television.

Therapist: Let's role-play appropriate listening. Pretend to be watching television again: Excuse me, would you please turn down the television so that I can talk to you?

Child: (*child looks at therapist*) Oh, I'm sorry, I didn't hear you.

Therapist: I just asked you to turn the television down so we can talk.

Child: Okay, the television is a little loud. (*Child pretends to turn the television down.*)

Therapist: Yeah, it's hard to compete with a good television show. Let's end the play here. Good job. You were able to demonstrate good listening. What did you do differently this time around?

Child: Well, I turned around and answered you when you said something. I turned down the TV

Therapist: You sure did. Anything else?

Child: I made good eye contact.

Therapist: You most certainly did. Your voice tone was also appropriate. You could have been angry or loud because I interrupted your television program, but you used appropriate voice tone.

In the above example, the therapist educates the child about the relationship between good listening and other basic social skills. More role-playing can be introduced during consecutive sessions to further demonstrate appropriate listening skills.

Nonverbal Communication. Nonverbal communication is a social skill that involves the use of gestures, body language, facial expressions, and other cues to express oneself other than by using speech or verbal expression as a form of communication. Nonverbal communication is also a higher level social skill that depends on eye contact and personal space. Although somewhat difficult to explain to a child, nonverbal communication often enhances verbal communication. So that the child fully understands this social skill, nonverbal cues or behaviors need to be emphasized. In this manual, I am primarily interested in educating children to become aware of nonverbal behaviors associated with feelings. The following dialogue may be helpful when explaining nonverbal communication to a child:

Therapist: Nonverbal communication is a social skill that we use every day. However, we may not be aware that we are using this skill when talking and interacting with others. Nonverbal communication is different from talking or using our voice to express ourselves, but it helps us when we talk with each other. Nonverbal communication means that we use our bodies to express our feelings when we are with other people. Since you already have learned a lot about eye contact, I will first teach you how we can communicate nonverbally with our eyes. Do you remember when we talked about using good eye contact?

Child: Yeah.

Therapist: Do you remember some of the important things we said about good eye contact?

Child: Yeah. You should look at people when you talk?

Therapist: Okay, but can you recall why?

Child: It shows that you're paying attention.

Therapist: You're correct. You already know that when people don't look at one another when they talk it may show that they're not interested or are avoiding each other. Our eyes can also help us express feelings. I'm going to pretend to communicate with you nonverbally by using my eyes. I want you to tell me what I am trying to say or do nonverbally, okay?

Child: Okay.

Therapist: (*Therapist stretches arms and yawns.*) What do you think this nonverbal message means?

Child: You're tired?

Therapist: Right. Now what am I communicating? (*Therapist closes eyes and pretends to be asleep.*)

Child: (*laughs*) You fell asleep.

Therapist: I was tired and fell asleep. You were able to see what I was doing even though I didn't talk or use my voice. I communicated with you nonverbally. People can also express feelings nonverbally. Do you remember the "Feelings Poster" that we used a while ago that showed faces of children expressing feelings? Their facial expressions showed many different feelings and emotions.

Child: I still have my poster.

Therapist: Good for you. Do you remember any of the feelings that were on the poster?

Child: Yeah. There was one where the boy looked really scared.

Therapist: Okay. We can tell how someone feels by looking at them. Pictures of people in books and magazines can help you identify feelings and nonverbal behavior. Now I'm going to show you another example of communicating nonverbally. (*Therapist drops head, begins to rub eyes, and pretends to make a sniffling sound.*)

Child: Now you're crying.

Therapist: How could you tell?

Child: You were wiping your eyes and you had your head down. You also sounded like you were crying.

Therapist: How do you think I was pretending to feel?

Child: Sad.

Therapist: How could you tell?

Child: Your face looked sad and you weren't looking at me. You were wiping your eyes.

Therapist: Good job. You were able to see that I was sad even though I didn't say anything to you. You could tell how I was feeling by my nonverbal gestures. Let's do some more examples of nonverbal communication. This time I want you to express your feelings or thoughts about something using nonverbal communication. What food do you hate the most?

Child: Peas and spinach.

Therapist: I want you to pretend that I just gave you a big dish of peas and spinach all mixed together for you to eat.

Child: Eww . . . Yucky.

Therapist: Show me how it's yucky without talking.

Child: (*Child frowns, sticks out tongue, and shakes head from left to right.*)

Therapist: (*laughs*) I believe you're trying to tell me that you don't like this food. Your face has a frown. You're shaking your head as if to tell me "No, please don't give me this food." You also were sticking your tongue out as if to say "gross." How did I do?

Child: Good!

Therapist: I was able to get a pretty good idea of what you thought and felt by watching your facial expression and nonverbal gestures. You didn't have to tell me with words or your voice, because I could see what you were communicating through your gestures. If you also use your voice at the same time that you use nonverbal skills, I'll get more information about your dislike of peas and spinach. Now I want you to pretend all over again, but this time I want you to express verbally your disgust at being given peas and spinach, okay?

Child: (*Child frowns, shakes head, and sticks out tongue.*) Eww . . . I hate peas and spinach. I don't want to eat this nasty food.

Therapist: (*laughs*) You convinced me. Remind me never to give you peas or spinach.

To be certain that the child has fully grasped the major points of nonverbal communication, you may use more examples. For example, you can ask the child to pretend to show anger nonverbally. If the child has difficulty dramatizing this emotion nonverbally, you can demonstrate anger by balling up fists and clenching teeth, or by glaring and stomping out of the room. Other emotions, such as sadness, fear, and happiness can also be demonstrated nonverbally to educate the child about this very important, and somewhat complex, social skill.

You should teach each skill in the same manner, as indicated through the following steps:

1. *Understand why the skill is important.* Emphasize to the child how every skill will be of value to him or her.

2. *Understand the skill by engaging in the skill.* Help the child master the skill by going over it several times.

3. *Practice the skill at home.* Encourage the child to practice the skill for a short time each day during specific situations.

4. *Practice the skill with others.* Encourage the child to practice the skill while in the presence of others in order to receive feedback about how well he or she is performing the skill. Through feedback, the child can learn to correct mistakes and obtain progress as to how well he or she is mastering the designated skill.

5. *Practice makes perfect.* Frequently encourage the child to practice each skill.

Feedback

The therapist obtains feedback from the child about his or her perceptions and understanding regarding the importance of appropriate social skills.

Creative Experiment

Instruct the child to practice social skills at least two times prior to the next session, particularly during interactions with two or more persons, such as in a group activity, school, or other public place.

For Group Therapy

Instruct the group to count off by twos. Group participants form two lines, ones on one side of the room and twos on the other facing their designated partner. Ask the children to stand about ten feet apart from their partners. Provide the following directions: You'll be directing them to act out inappropriate social skills:

Listen carefully to the instructions I am about to give you. This exercise is called "Therapist Says" and is similar to Simon Says. I'll start with an example: Therapist says, raise both arms above your head. Therapist says, put them down.

After I give you a specific instruction, you will demonstrate or act out what I just asked you to do. I'll then ask you to tell me by using a thumbs up sign if the behavior was appropriate. If the behavior was inappropriate give me a thumbs down sign. Are you ready? Okay, first direction: Therapist says, walk toward your partner (*children should walk very close to each other before being told to stop*). Therapist says stop—appropriate or inappropriate? (*Children should use thumbs down sign.*)

Encourage the children to share feelings and thoughts about why they considered an interaction to be inappropriate. You can use many other examples to depict social skills deficits.

At the end of this group exercise, encourage children to provide feedback about their thoughts and feelings.

You may also use appropriate social skills in the Therapist Says exercise.

CHAPTER FOURTEEN

Session XI:
Inventory of Thoughts

Objective: To teach the child to recognize automatic negative thoughts in order to learn to prevent them

Introduction

Briefly review social skills, including the child's response to the creative experiment.

Agenda

- Review automatic negative thoughts (bad self-talk) and rational positive thoughts (good self-talk).

- Demonstrate these concepts via examples.

- Encourage the child to identify automatic negative thoughts that may occur spontaneously or when a problem or conflict arises on a daily basis.

- Ask the child to identify rational positive thoughts that may enhance self-esteem on a daily basis.

- Discuss specific issues or concerns identified by the child.

Presentation/Exercise

By this time the child should be able to identify two of the most important concepts of cognitive therapy, automatic negative thoughts and rational positive thoughts. Emphasize that positive thoughts are those that have a positive, feel-good effect on your mood, for example, "I do well in school," "I'm honest," "My family loves me," "My schoolwork is great," and "I have nice friends." On the other hand, the child may remember that negative thoughts are those thoughts that have a bad effect on mood, usually because they focus on the bad points, for example, "I'm no good," "I can't do anything right," "My friends no longer want me around," and "My teacher thinks I'm stupid."

During this session, give the child ten to fifteen minutes in which to come up with any current automatic negative thoughts about himself or herself. The following dialogue shows how you may go about conducting a brainstorming session in which you ask the child to identify automatic negative thoughts, or bad self-talk:

Therapist: We've been working for some time on how to see when you're experiencing automatic negative thoughts, or bad self-talk. You've also learned how to replace this kind of talk with more rational positive thoughts, or good self-talk. You've done a good job so far in catching yourself when negative self-talk occurs. Now we are at the point in your therapy where we'll be completing the twelve-session cognitive therapy program. Usually when children have gotten this far and have done as well as you have, we therapists would like to make sure that you're prepared to continue to monitor your thoughts and feelings outside of these sessions. Today, I'm going to help you come up with a list of positive thoughts, or good self-talk, that you can use when a problem situation occurs. You can refer to these thoughts whenever an automatic negative thought pops up for you. Before we talk about good self-talk, let's brainstorm some of the bad self-talk that commonly occurs for you and may come up in the future. For you to be able to feel good, it's essential for you to remember to practice brainstorming for your "Inventory of Thoughts." It'll be important for you to go through this brainstorming technique for ten to fifteen minutes each time you feel down, angry, or depressed. Let's practice brainstorming together.

Child: Okay.

Therapist: Can you recall any of the automatic negative thoughts you often experienced when things didn't work out or when a problem came up?

Child: Yeah! I always say, "I'm stupid or no good," but I know that I'm not.

Therapist: You're right, you're not, but that when things happen we often think this way. You're able to identify that you say, "I am stupid and no good" as automatic negative thoughts that pop into your head when a problem situation occurs. Do you recall any other automatic thoughts or bad self-talk that you've said to yourself?

Child: No one likes me. Nothing good ever works out for me.

Therapist: Great, you have done a good job in identifying your commonly experienced negative thoughts. I can tell that the earlier sessions in which we talked about identifying bad self-talk have helped you recall some of the common negative statements you've made when you were feeling upset, sad, down, or angry. Now let's look at some of the questions you can ask yourself outside these sessions when a problem occurs that brings about bad self-talk. Right now it's easier for you because we have been working a long time on this. So what kind of questions can you ask yourself that will help identify these thoughts?

Child: Well, that's easy. I can say, "Why am I putting myself down? What happened to make me start thinking like this?"

Therapist: That's good. These kinds of questions can help you look at the situation more realistically because the problem or situation that you just experienced may not be as bad as you thought. Asking yourself these types of questions, like "Why am I putting myself down?" or "What happened to make me start thinking like this?" can help you identify your bad self-talk.

This type of brainstorming exercise will better enable you to understand the child's dysfunctional beliefs. Thus, you will be able to determine if the child may have some thoughts that are more disturbing than others. The child is instructed to write down these thoughts on an index card.

After this task is completed, ask the child to share his or her card with you. Help the child to make a list of the most important positive thoughts that reflect his or her character. This exercise will be referred to as the "Inventory of Thoughts." Emphasize that the list of positive thoughts is more important, because it can be used as a self-esteem booster whenever the child feels sad, depressed, angry, and so on.

Note: Refer to the following example to further clarify the "Inventory of Thoughts" exercise.

Automatic Negative Thoughts (bad self-talk)	**Rational Positive Thoughts** (good self-talk)
My teacher thinks I'm stupid.	I'm not stupid. I get good grades when I study.
My friends no longer want me around.	I have a few friends that play with me.
I can't do anything right.	Everybody makes mistakes and besides, I do a lot of things okay.
No one loves me.	When my mom gives me hugs, it means that she loves me.
I'm no good.	I'm an okay kid.

The following dialogue provides an example of a therapist helping a child find rational positive responses (good self-talk):

Therapist: We've already practiced how to identify automatic negative thoughts, or bad self-talk. You remember that the main point of cognitive therapy is to help you learn how to substitute your automatic negative thoughts by using rational positive thoughts, or good self-talk. We know that it's often easier to identify our automatic negative thoughts, but it's a bigger challenge to continue on your own, when therapy is completed, and without my help, to identify the positive rational thoughts. So, today let's make a game of it, so you're more likely to remember how to replace any future bad self-talk with good self-talk.

Child: Okay.

Therapist: One of your most commonly experienced automatic negative thoughts has been "I'm stupid," right?

Child: Yeah, but I don't say I'm stupid that much anymore.

Therapist: I know. You've learned how to change this type of talk when it occurs. However, if you do have that type of thought again, what questions could you ask yourself that would help you replace the negative thought with a statement or thought that is more realistic and positive—in other words, a thought that will make you feel better about yourself? Let's pretend that a situation occurred and you had the automatic negative thought "I'm stupid." What do you say to yourself to change this?

Child: I'm not stupid!

Therapist: Okay, I agree. But how do you convince yourself that you're not stupid?

Child: I would say to myself that I get good grades when I study. I got an A on my English test. I don't fail any classes. My friends don't call me stupid.

Therapist: Okay, good job. So, what process did you just use to convince yourself that your first automatic thought of "I'm stupid" is incorrect?

Child: I talked to myself!

Therapist: Yeah, but what else did you do?

Child: I remember: I questioned myself, right?

Therapist: Exactly. You examined the evidence, checking it out to see if what you're saying to yourself about the situation is actually true or not. You asked yourself, "What other reasons could there be for the situation" as well as "what if" questions. It'll be helpful for you to remember these questions because they'll help you find rational positive thoughts. Remember also that making positive remarks like self-affirmations and coping statements can also be a helpful way of identifying good self-talk that will ultimately lead you to feel better.

By the completion of this session, the child has become quite skilled at identifying when he or she is experiencing bad self-talk and has learned how to effectively replace the negative thoughts with good self-talk. It's important for you to explain to the child that all people—adults and children of all ages—experience negative thoughts from time to time and that it's unrealistic to expect to never have another negative thought. What is most important is that the child continue to identify and replace the negative thoughts with more positive rational responses. Teaching the child to brainstorm independently will help him or her continue to keep negative thoughts in check, which in turn will help maintain mood stabilization.

For Group Therapy

Draw two columns on a chalkboard or large chart. One column is bad self-talk and the other is good self-talk. Ask group members to brainstorm the most commonly expressed negative statements (bad self-talk) reported during the course of group treatment. Write down the statements as they are being expressed. After this brainstorming exercise, ask the children to challenge these negative statements with rational responses (good self-talk). Write these statements on the board as well. Follow with a group discussion.

Feedback

Try to elicit thoughts and feelings from the child about today's session.

Creative Experiment

Give the child the "Inventory of Thoughts Record" to complete prior to next session. The child should write thoughts down on the sheet whenever they occur. Also ask the child to identify two or three personal problem situations that have consistently been defined as repetitive negative themes throughout previous sessions.

Inventory of Thoughts Record

Name_____   **Date**_____

Automatic Negative Thoughts "Bad Self Talk"	Rational Positive Thoughts "Good Self Talk"

CHAPTER FIFTEEN

Session XII:
You Feel Good

Objective: To prepare the child to continue this type of thinking on his or her own after therapy is over

Introduction

Briefly review the last session, including the "Inventory of Thoughts Record," as well as an overview of cognitive therapy concepts, with emphasis primarily on automatic negative thoughts and rational positive thoughts and how these concepts relate to depressed mood.

Agenda

- Ask the child to present two or three personal problem situations that have been defined as repetitive negative themes throughout previous sessions.

- Help the child identify and further clarify these themes using "Enemy Camp vs. Enemy Destroyers" index cards.

- Discuss specific issues or concerns identified by the child.

Presentation/Exercise

In collaboration with the child, identify and define at least two or three problem situations that have been addressed consistently throughout the sessions. These situations are those that often cause negative thinking in the child's daily life, such as school-related difficulties, poor peer relationships, sibling conflicts, family pressure, and so on. After the child identifies problem situations, he or she will then write each situation on a separate index card.

The child will also write down those negative thoughts that come to mind each time the situation is experienced. On the opposite side of the flash card, the child will then write rational positive responses to the negative thoughts. The goal of this exercise is to challenge and replace negative thoughts. Encourage the child to practice these positive thoughts using the index cards whenever necessary. After the exercise is completed, praise the child for earning the title of Mr. or Ms. Feel Good.

You can also develop Coping Cards with the child during this final session. These cards will only have positive self-statements on them and will help him or her handle future difficult situations.

For Group Therapy

A party should be planned for the final group session. Ask the children to provide suggestions regarding activities and games, and encourage them to bring snacks. During this session, encourage participants to discuss their thoughts and feelings about termination. You may want to discuss separation issues in this final session. Encourage the children to share their perceptions about any progress they feel they've made during the course of treatment. You can start the sharing process by telling each child something positive that occurred as a result of being a group participant. It is also important to discuss your own feelings regarding group termination.

Throughout the group process, the children have become accustomed to sharing their thoughts and feelings in the presence of others; therefore, they should be prepared to receive feedback from you and the other participants regarding progress made toward treatment goals. Children who you feel have not been successful in meeting treatment goals should be seen during an individual session prior to termination. During this individual session, address specific recommendations (individual booster sessions, participation in next scheduled group) with the child and his or her parents.

Final Good-Bye exercise: Encourage the children to say good-bye and to share personal coping statements that they found to be helpful. They can share their Coping Cards with the others before saying their final good-byes.

Feedback

During the remainder of the session, address termination issues and try to elicit from the child his or her overall perceptions of the sessions.

Creative Experiment

Instruct the child to take home index cards and/or Coping Cards to use whenever problems arise. Encourage the child to practice the creative experiments that have been most beneficial during the course of the therapy sessions.

CHAPTER SIXTEEN

Conclusion

This manual is based on a collaborative relationship between child and therapist. It focuses on enhancing the child's self-esteem by alleviating depressive symptoms and instilling the value of using good self-talk. The specific interventions included may require adaptation for each child due to differences in age and personal problems and stressors. Keep in mind that the major ingredients to use when working with all children are flexibility, patience, creativity, spontaneity, and humor.

References

Asarnow, J. R., and G. A. Carlson. 1988. "Childhood Depression: Five Year Outcome Following Combined Cognitive-Behavior Therapy and Pharmacotherapy." *American Journal of Psychotherapy*, 62.

Beck, A.T. 1978. *Depression Inventory*. Philadelphia: Center for Cognitive Therapy.

———. 1976. *Cognitive Therapy and the Emotional Disorders*. New York: International Universities Press.

Beck, A. T., A. J. Rush, B. F. Shaw, et al. 1979. *Cognitive Therapy of Depression*. New York: Guilford Press.

Bedrosian, R. C. 1981. "The Application of Cognitive Therapy Techniques with Adolescents," in *New Direction in Cognitive Therapy: A Casebook*. G. Emery, S. D. Hollon, and R. C. Bedrosian, (eds.). New York: Guilford Press.

Bernstein, D. A., and T. D. Borkovec. 1973. *Progressive Relaxation: A Manual for Therapists*. Illinois: Research Press.

Birmaher, B., et al. 1996. "Childhood and Adolescent Depression: A Review of the Past Ten Years. Part One." *Journal of the American Academy of Child and Adolescent Psychiatry.*

———. In press, 1996. "Childhood and Adolescent Depression: A Review of the Past Ten Years. Part Two." *Journal of the American Academy of Child and Adolescent Psychiatry.*

Blackburn, I. M., S. Bishop, A. I. M. Glen. 1981. "The Efficacy of Cognitive Therapy in Depression: A Treatment Trial Using Cognitive Therapy and Pharmacotherapy, Each Alone and in Combination." *British Journal of Psychiatry*, 139:181–189.

Bowers, W. A. 1989. "Cognitive Therapy With Inpatients," in *Comprehensive Handbook of Cognitive Therapy*. Freeman, A., K. M. Simon, et al. (eds.). New York: Plenum Press.

Brent, D. A. 1989. *Cognitive Therapy Manual*. Pittsburgh, PA: Western Psychiatric Institute and Clinic.

Brown, R. A., and P. M. Lewinsohn. 1984. "A Psychoeducational Approach to the Treatment of Depression: Comparison of Group, Individual and Minimal Contact Procedures." *Journal of Consulting and Clinical Psychology*, 52:174–183.

Burns, D. D. 1989. *The Feeling Good Handbook*. New York: William Morrow Co., Inc.

Burns, D. D. 1980. *Feeling Good, The New Mood Therapy*. New York: William Morrow Co., Inc.

Costello, C. G. 1981. "Childhood Depression," in *Behavioral Assessment of Childhood Disorders*. E. J. Mash and L. J. Terdal (eds.). New York: Guilford Press.

Covi, L., and L. Primakoff. 1988. "Cognitive Group Therapy," in *Review of Psychiatry*. A. J. Frances, and R. E. Hales (eds.). Washington, DC: American Psychiatric Press.

DiGiusseppe, R. A. 1981. "Cognitive Therapy with Children" in *New Directions in Cognitive Therapy: A Casebook*. G. Emery, S. D. Hollon, and R. C. Bedrosian (eds.). New York: Guilford Press.

Ellis, A. 1982. "Rational Emotive Group Therapy," in *Basic Approaches to Group Therapy and Group Counseling*. G. M. Gazda (ed.). Springfield, IL: Charles C. Thomas.

Ellis, A. and J. Whiteley, eds. 1979. *Theoretical and Empirical Foundations of Rational Emotive Therapy*. Pacific Grove, CA: Brooks/Cole Publishing Co.

Emery, G., S. D. Holden and R. C. Bedrosian. 1981. *New Directions in Cognitive Therapy: A Casebook*. New York: Guilford Press.

Frame, C. L., and M. E. Cuddy. 1989. "Affective Disorders," in *Innovations in Child Behavior Therapy*. M. Hersen (ed.). New York: Springer.

Freeman, et al. eds. 1989. "Cognitive Therapy with Inpatients." *Comprehensive Handbook of Cognitive Therapy*. New York: Plenum Press.

Garber, J., and R. Hilsman. 1992. "Cognitions, Stress, and Depression in Children and Adolescents." *Child and Adolescent Psychiatric Clinics of North America*, 8.

Hollon, S. D., and B. F. Shaw. 1979. "Group Cognitive Therapy for Depressed Patients," in *Cognitive Therapy for Depression*. A. T. Beck, A. J. Rush, B. F. Shaw, et al. (eds.). New York: Guilford Press.

Kaplan. C. A., A. E. Thompson, and S. M. Searson. 1995. "Cognitive Behavior Therapy in Children and Adolescents." *Archives of Disease in Childhood*. 73:472–475.

Keepers, T. D. 1987. "Group Treatment of Children: Practical Considerations and Techniques," in *Innovations in Clinical Practice: A Source Book*. P. A. Keller and S. R. Heyman (eds.). Florida: Professional Resource Exchange, Inc.

Kendall, P. C. (ed.). 1991. *Child and Adolescent Therapy: Cognitive Behavioral Procedures*. New York: Guilford Press.

Kovacs, M. 1992. "Childhood Depression Inventory (CDI)." North Tonawanda: Multi Health Systems.

———. 1996. "Presentation and Course of Major Depression Disorder During Childhood and Later Years of The Life Span."*Journal of the American Academy of Child and Adolescent Psychiatry*, 35(6):705–715.

Kovacs, M., T. L. Feinberg, and M. Crouse-Novak. 1984. "Depressive Disorders in Childhood: I. A Longitudinal Prospective Study of Characteristics and Recovery." *Archives of General Psychiatry*, 41:229–237.

Kovacs, M., T. L. Feinberg and M. Crouse-Novak. 1984. "Depressive Disorders in Childhood: II. A Longitudinal Study of the Risk for a Subsequent Major Depression." *Archives of General Psychiatry*, 41:643–649.

Kramer, P., and L. Frazer. 1985. *The Dynamics of Relationships*. Florida: Kids' Rights.

Lewinsohn, P. M. 1978. *Control Your Depression*. New Jersey: Prentice Hall, Inc.

Meichenbaum, D. 1977. *Cognitive Behavior Modification: An Integrative Approach*. New York: Plenum Press.

Nissen, G. 1986. "Treatment for Depression in Children and Adolescents." *Psychopathology, 19:* 156–161.

Piers, E. V., and D. B. Harris. 1969. "Age and Other Correlates of Self-Concept in Children." *Journal of Educational Psychology*. 5:91–95.

Poling, K. 1989. *Living With Depression: A Survival Manual for Families*. Pittsburgh, PA: Western Psychiatric Institute and Clinic.

Puig, A. J., and W. Chambers. 1978. "The Schedule for Affective Disorders and Schizophrenia for School-Age Children (Kiddie-SADS)." New York: New York State Psychiatric Institute.

Reynolds, W. M., and K. I. Coats. 1986. "A Comparison of Cognitive Behavioral Therapy and Relaxation Training for the Treatment of Depression in Adolescents." *Journal of Consulting and Clinical Psychology*, 54:653–660.

Reynolds, W. R. 1988. "Major Depression," in *Child Behavior Therapy Casebook*. M. Hersen and C. G. Last (eds.). New York: Plenum Press.

Rose, S. D., S. Tolman, and S. Tallent. 1985. "Group Process in Cognitive Behavioral Therapy." *Behavior Therapist*, 8:71–75.

Rush, J. 1994. *Cognitive Therapy For Depressed Adolescents*. New York: Guilford Press.

Russo, J. T. 1986. "Cognitive Counseling for Adolescents." *Journal of Child and Adolescent Psychotherapy*, 3:194–198.

Ryan, N. 1987. "Depression in Children and Adolescents." STAR Center Link, Western Psychiatric Institute and Clinic.

Spence, S. 1994. "Practitioner Review: Cognitive Therapy with Children and Adolescents—From Theory to Practice." *Journal of Child Psychology and Psychiatry*, 35, no. 7.

Spivack, G., J. Platt, and M. Shure. 1976. *The Problem-Solving Approach to Adjustment*. San Francisco: Jossey-Bass.

Stark, K. D., W. M. Reynolds, and N. J. Kaslow. 1987. "A Comparison of the Relative Efficacy of Self-Control Therapy and a Behavioral Problem-Solving Therapy for Depression in Children." *Journal of Abnormal Child Psychology*, 15, no. 1.

Stark, K. D., L. W. Rouse, and R. Livingstone. 1991. "Treatment of Depression During Childhood and Adolescence: Cognitive-Behavioral Procedures for the Individual and Family," in *Child and Adolescent Therapy-Cognitive-Behavioral Procedures*. P. C. Kendall (ed.). New York: Guilford Press.

Ubell, E. 1986. "Is That Child Bad or Depressed?" *Parade Magazine*.

Weinberg, W. A., et al. 1973. "Depression in Children Referred to an Educational Diagnostic Center: Diagnosis and Treatment." *Journal of Pediatrics*, 83.

Weissberg, R. P., E. L. Gesten, and N. Schmid. 1980. *The Rochester Social Problem Solving (SPS) Program: A Training Manual for Teachers of 2nd–4th Grade Children*. Primary Mental Health Project, Center for Community Study, Rochester, NY.

Wilkes, T. C. R., and J. Rush. 1988. "Adaptations of Cognitive Therapy for Depressed Adolescents." *Journal of the American Academy of Child and Adolescent Psychiatry*, 381–386.

Wright, J. H., and G. R. Schrodt. 1987. "Inpatient Treatment of Adolescents," in *Cognitive Therapy: Applications in Psychiatric and Medical Settings*. A. Freeman, and V. Greenwood, (eds.). New York: Human Sciences Press.

Dear Reader,

Treating Depressed Children was developed as a means to help mental health professionals utilize cognitive therapy concepts creatively. I hope this manual will provide you with the necessary tools to effectively treat depressive symptoms in children and adolescents.

Sincerely,

Charma D. Dudley Ph.D.

For information on ordering additional copies of the Creative Experiments, please write to the following address:

Charma D. Dudley, Ph.D.
1739 East Carson Street
Box 233
Pittsburgh, PA 15203

Charma D. Dudley, Ph.D., SPPR, is a licensed psychologist, consultant, and trainer in Pittsburgh, Pennsylvania. Dr. Dudley specializes in the treatment of children and adolescents with depressive illnesses and behavioral problems. She has also held positions in several community-based mental health programs, and inpatient and outpatient psychiatric treatment settings in Pittsburgh and the surrounding areas.

Other New Harbinger Self-Help Titles

Preparing for Surgery, $17.95
Coming Out Everyday, $13.95
Ten Things Every Parent Needs to Know, $12.95
The Power of Two, $12.95
It's Not OK Anymore, $13.95
The Daily Relaxer, $12.95
The Body Image Workbook, $17.95
Living with ADD, $17.95
Taking the Anxiety Out of Taking Tests, $12.95
The Taking Charge of Menopause Workbook, $17.95
Living with Angina, $12.95
PMS: Women Tell Women How to Control Premenstrual Syndrome, $13.95
Five Weeks to Healing Stress: The Wellness Option, $17.95
Choosing to Live: How to Defeat Suicide Through Cognitive Therapy, $12.95
Why Children Misbehave and What to Do About It, $14.95
Illuminating the Heart, $13.95
When Anger Hurts Your Kids, $12.95
The Addiction Workbook, $17.95
The Mother's Survival Guide to Recovery, $12.95
The Chronic Pain Control Workbook, Second Edition, $17.95
Fibromyalgia & Chronic Myofascial Pain Syndrome, $19.95
Diagnosis and Treatment of Sociopaths, $44.95
Flying Without Fear, $12.95
Kid Cooperation: How to Stop Yelling, Nagging & Pleading and Get Kids to Cooperate, $12.95
The Stop Smoking Workbook: Your Guide to Healthy Quitting, $17.95
Conquering Carpal Tunnel Syndrome and Other Repetitive Strain Injuries, $17.95
The Tao of Conversation, $12.95
Wellness at Work: Building Resilience for Job Stress, $17.95
What Your Doctor Can't Tell You About Cosmetic Surgery, $13.95
An End to Panic: Breakthrough Techniques for Overcoming Panic Disorder, $17.95
On the Clients Path: A Manual for the Practice of Solution-Focused Therapy, $39.95
Living Without Procrastination: How to Stop Postponing Your Life, $12.95
Goodbye Mother, Hello Woman: Reweaving the Daughter Mother Relationship, $14.95
Letting Go of Anger: The 10 Most Common Anger Styles and What to Do About Them, $12.95
Messages: The Communication Skills Workbook, Second Edition, $13.95
Coping With Chronic Fatigue Syndrome: Nine Things You Can Do, $12.95
The Anxiety & Phobia Workbook, Second Edition, $17.95
Thueson's Guide to Over-the-Counter Drugs, $13.95
Natural Women's Health: A Guide to Healthy Living for Women of Any Age, $13.95
I'd Rather Be Married: Finding Your Future Spouse, $13.95
The Relaxation & Stress Reduction Workbook, Fourth Edition, $17.95
Living Without Depression & Manic Depression: A Workbook for Maintaining Mood Stability, $17.95
Coping With Schizophrenia: A Guide For Families, $13.95
Visualization for Change, Second Edition, $13.95
Postpartum Survival Guide, $13.95
Angry All the Time: An Emergency Guide to Anger Control, $12.95
Couple Skills: Making Your Relationship Work, $13.95
Handbook of Clinical Psychopharmacology for Therapists, $39.95
Weight Loss Through Persistence, $13.95
Post-Traumatic Stress Disorder: A Complete Treatment Guide, $39.95
Stepfamily Realities: How to Overcome Difficulties and Have a Happy Family, $13.95
The Chemotherapy Survival Guide, $11.95
The Deadly Diet, Second Edition: Recovering from Anorexia & Bulimia, $13.95
Last Touch: Preparing for a Parent's Death, $11.95
Self-Esteem, Second Edition, $13.95
I Can't Get Over It, A Handbook for Trauma Survivors, Second Edition, $15.95
Concerned Intervention, When Your Loved One Won't Quit Alcohol or Drugs, $12.95
Dying of Embarrassment: Help for Social Anxiety and Social Phobia, $12.95
The Depression Workbook: Living With Depression and Manic Depression, $17.95
Prisoners of Belief: Exposing & Changing Beliefs that Control Your Life, $12.95
Men & Grief: A Guide for Men Surviving the Death of a Loved One, $13.95
When the Bough Breaks: A Helping Guide for Parents of Sexually Abused Children, $11.95
When Once Is Not Enough: Help for Obsessive Compulsives, $13.95
The Three Minute Meditator, Third Edition, $12.95
Beyond Grief: A Guide for Recovering from the Death of a Loved One, $13.95
Leader's Guide to the Relaxation & Stress Reduction Workbook, Fourth Edition, $19.95
The Divorce Book, $13.95
Hypnosis for Change: A Manual of Proven Techniques, Third Edition, $13.95
When Anger Hurts, $13.95
Lifetime Weight Control, $12.95

Call **toll free, 1-800-748-6273,** to order. Have your Visa or Mastercard number ready. Or send a check for the titles you want to New Harbinger Publications, Inc., 5674 Shattuck Ave., Oakland, CA 94609. Include $3.80 for the first book and 75¢ for each additional book, to cover shipping and handling. (California residents please include appropriate sales tax.) Allow four to six weeks for delivery.

Prices subject to change without notice.